THE AMERICAN DEMAGOGUE

I0091449

Dedication
To
Arthur and Lillie Smith,
whose descendants continue to cover the earth.

THE AMERICAN DEMAGOGUE

Donald Trump

Revised and Updated Edition

Molefi Kete Asante

Universal Write Publications, LLC

New York, NY

THE AMERICAN DEMAGOGUE: DONALD TRUMP

Revised and Updated Edition

ISBN: 978-0-9742269-0-3

Printed in the United States of America.

Mailing/Submissions:

Universal Write Publications, LLC
421 8th avenue, Suite 86
New York, NY 10116

Website: UWPBooks.com

This book has been partially supported with a financial grant from SAGE Publishing.

S Sage

Contents

Acknowledgments

I want to thank my publisher, Dr. Ayo Sekai, whose dedication to academic publishing has become one of the heroic tests of resilience in a world full of competition for recognition of good work. She has been devoted to making Universal Write Publications a company of skilled editors and authors who will change the nature of Afrocentric scholarship. May this book, and many others, be added to this line in the interest of unfettered rational thought.

Preface

Demagogues tend to be the same across generations and countries, and in this book, I attempt to show how Donald Trump in any guise is no more than a petty demagogue whose acclaimed narcissism and socio-pathology are similar to those of other demagogues. Clearly, the rise of Trump to the presidency of the United States signaled the radical abandonment by the American electorate of the long arc of progress that had become the hallmark of every president since Franklin Roosevelt, Democrat or Republican. Trump took up the politics of fear, the rhetoric of intimidation, and the temperament of a bully in his relationships with members of his own government, his opponents, and other world leaders.

No person ever attained the presidency with such anti-institutional bias as Donald Trump. His attack on the security institutions, the FBI (Federal Bureau of Investigation) and the CIA (Central Intelligence Agency) specifically, was crass and mean-spirited, and his attempt to shut down the media institutions that did not support his presidency was frighteningly similar to the way the German *Regenpropagandaministerium* under Hitler and Goebbels attempted to control information during the Third Reich.

Trump, like Hitler, took his rhetoric of fear to the social media of the day to persuade the millions who could listen to him or read him without the important critiques of experienced media commentators. Like other demagogues, Trump understood that control of the security and media institutions was central to his ability to dominate the imagination of a nation. Trump would do this by employing the platform given to him by the Alt-Right, Fox News Agency, and Breitbart to spread his version of fear, hatred, enemy opposition, and messianic delivery. It is necessary for those who understand the decline of civility, the abhorrence of reason, and the whipping up of mean-spirited emotions to speak truth to authority and challenge hatred with concern and care. Demagogues do not get better or more civil; they demand more attention, power, and control. Speaking against such a decline in society is what the conscious intellectual must do.

When Trump addressed his rallies during the election campaign of 2015 for the presidency, he had the instrumental support of the Russians, who worked to elect him president of the United States. All of these rallies were followed by his bold and racist announcement of his candidacy at Trump Tower on June 16, 2015, when he said,

> When Mexico sends its people, they're not sending their best. They're not sending you. They're not sending you. They're sending people that have lots of problems, and they're bringing those problems with us. They're bringing drugs. They're bringing crime. They're rapists. And some, I assume, are good people.

This is widely believed to have been Trump's signal to what would become his political base, the white racist population that hated the integrated, diverse, and multiracial country the United States had become. Regardless of whatever he would say in the coming weeks and months, this quote would never be corrected, changed, or modified by Trump. It would follow him as surely as ants would follow the path to sugar. He was not just stuck with the words; he wanted the words to be his so that he could use them as bait to bring in those who felt they needed, after former president Barack Obama, a white savior. But, of course, saviors do not come without a cost to national morality, the bruising of core values, and the demise of free speech.

What Trump meant was that he was the One, when he said,

> Now, our country needs—our country needs a truly great leader, and we need a truly great leader now. We need a leader that wrote *The Art of the Deal*. We need a leader that can bring back our jobs, can bring back our manufacturing, can bring back our military, can take care of our vets. Our vets have been abandoned. And we also need a cheerleader.

Most truly great leaders do not announce their greatness; it is bestowed on them by history. Only the truly fearful, the insecure, the jealous, the bitter, and the misguided resort to bluster, bombast, and a penchant for control of all institutions. By exploiting the weaknesses of those surrounding the "Leader," Trump is able to find obsequiousness in the obvious suppliants who seek closeness to power. Those who have vulnerabilities, that is, those who are threatened in any intellectual or moral capacity, become the pallets on which the demagogue lays his trust because they have been considered not smart, dirty, easily tempted to corruption, or incompetent. Rising to work in the interest of the Leader, they become a cadre of promoters who vow to feed the ego of the demagogue. They will often stick around so long as they are subservient, praise the most stupid actions of the demagogue, and do not feel frustrated by his personal insults. To the degree that the demagogue's base becomes like the demagogue, they have neither integrity nor character.

I have written this book because I have faith in the inexorable nature of people power, and I believe that it is possible to stop "he-who-would-become-the-Leader" by the rising up of the masses who refuse to be dictated to by any person who rides roughshod over democratic processes. As an African American, I have had to believe in the ordinary people, attached to laws and to a certain degree of morality and common interest in peaceful coexistence that would sustain the movement toward justice by underwriting a national commitment to equality of all people.

In 2023, as I write this revised edition, Trump, impeached twice, indicted for serious crimes, and convicted so far twice, has maintained his attraction to about 30% of the American electorate. His clamor for the presidency again is no different from the first Trump campaign, although this time he has added his own personal grievances to the list that he had in 2015. He claims that the election of 2020 was stolen, although there is no evidence that this is true. In fact, the courts rejected these false claims, and Trump and others were indicted in Fulton County, Georgia, on a racketeering charge for seeking to overthrow the election of Joseph Biden to the presidency. They had all participated in a conspiracy to have former vice president Mike Pence refuse to certify the election on January 6, 2020. When Pence refused, Trump's supporters overran the Capitol building, ransacked offices, and shouted, "Hang Mike Pence!" Fortunately, they were unable to find the vice president.

Biden and Kamala Harris, as president and vice president, entered the White House in January 2020 to lead the nation toward a more stable and regular government. Biden's campaign was designed to lower the bombast and to bring to order the chaos that had accompanied the previous presidency. Trump's narcissistic bombast dominated the news cycle of the United States for several years, including the years when he was not president. Stumbling toward a regular order, the people of the nation have fought to reinforce institutions and to claim an agenda in support of the aspirations of a multicultural democracy.

INTRODUCTION

Perhaps no American presidential campaign or presidency has been contorted with as much anti-American rhetoric as the campaign of 2015 and the presidency of Donald Trump beginning in 2016. I mean, I do not recall a candidate who has taken on the memes, core values, representative institutions, and optimism that are usually associated with the American nation and turned them into such negations of promise as has Trump. There is no question that the Trump experience will be seen as a pivotal project where the deep continuity of a nation was fractured by a wildly unique and wily politician who capitalized on his television celebrity to bend the nation toward moral deformity for political purposes. What one wonders is whether or not Trump knew that humanity was dirtier, meaner, and eviler than others knew.

In many ways, Trump is the anti-American, the twisted and distorted version of what an American was thought to be. Indeed, if one thought of Americans as being progressive in their relationship to the pollution of the Earth, then Trump says pollution is good. If you thought of Americans as proactive against racism and racial injustice, then Trump proves that some on the side of racism are good. If you understood Americans to be open to the weak, the hungry, and the poor, then Trump proves that he does not have the same compassion demonstrated by other presidents, either Republican or Democrat. One can select any set of American institutions, either security or media, for example, and in each case, Trump has demonstrated an easy ability to bash those institutions or organizations he views as opposed to his brand of politics.

Consequently, my objective in this book, given my background as a scholar in the field of communication and as an Africologist with an eye toward the negative images, symbols, language, and references used by Trump to denounce his predecessors, especially President Barack Obama, was to reveal the dirty underbelly of an American demagogue who peddles lies as his political bargaining chips.

Many years ago, one of my former students at the University of Buffalo, Erika Vora, wrote a dissertation on the subject of diffusion of information using some of the rhetorical addresses of Adolf Hitler as the basic documents. What I learned from reading Vora's study was that the demagogue could effectively turn the ordinary citizen into an angry, irrational, and violent votarist simply by using lies, appeals to fear, and suggestions that one would lose a job, a spouse, or a child by allowing "foreigners" to enter the country. Trump pulled out every instrument of persuasion at his disposal to obliterate rational thinking from the very first day of his presidency when he and his people claimed that they had a larger crowd at his inauguration than was present at Obama's inauguration. It was a large lie, an in-your-face, bold lie that caught most people off guard. During the next few days, Trump established a pattern of dominating the news cycle with a tweet a day, sometimes several tweets a day, and then watching the commentators, news anchors, and general population discuss his latest lie. Hitler had tried to do a similar thing with radio; indeed, his was the first real radio demagoguery. Trump resorted to Twitter, using it to create a topic line for the day, thus truncating any other line that might interfere with his visibility in the media.

Democracies are governments by rational argument. The United States of America has often been described as "the leader of the free world," where government by talk, not by fear, bullying, or lies, dominates the public sphere. When I felt that this tradition was under threat, I decided it was necessary to revisit the making of a demagogue. One could have talked in the past about American politicians being racist, ignorant, misogynist, or segregationists, but no one had reached the height that Trump reached with a ranting, ignorant, lying behavior simply by appealing to the worst instincts of human beings. According to Trump, if you felt that your opponents were not human, then you could "knock the crap" out of them. If you felt that Mexicans would not be good judges, then you would try to avoid Mexican judges.

In this book, I intend to examine how fear is used to create radical anti-immigration and anti-foreign feelings. But this is not enough to make a demagogue; it was necessary for Trump to also tackle the most appreciated, loved, and respected individuals of the society. By demeaning their intelligence, downplaying their achievements, and damaging their reputations with his lies, he re-created himself in the image of a singularly unique and special leader who could correct the deeds of the past. Trump would challenge the popular Obama by continuing the assault on his origins and being coy about whether now he would admit the evidence that Obama was born in Hawaii. He had circulated the lie prior to his election, and those who believed him, so gullible were they and so needy for a savior, accepted the lie as if Trump had been at Fatima and had seen something that no one else could have seen. The energy that he put into attacking Obama was the kind of venom many black people have experienced in America. It was personal, gloomy, and disturbing in its vileness, and it carried with it an existential threat to the name and person of Obama. Many people thought that Trump's attitude toward Obama's presidency bordered on a hateful jealousy of Obama. Nothing Obama said or did could be entertained by Trump; his animus was clouded by a small ego writ large by insisting that he was someone other than who he was: a Queens, New York, man who had inherited millions from his father to begin his career. He would have cabinet officers vow to take down all Obama-era reforms and regulations, almost gutting the Environmental Protection Agency by making it an agency that protected not the people but the large corporations. Health care was tangled into a web where individuals lost their ability to survive in times of crisis; Trump's attitude added to the uncertainty and existential threat that many sick people felt.

Although Trump peddled fear, he was mortally frightened by the possibility of losing the election to Hillary Clinton. She was the most qualified person to ever run for the office, having served as First Lady for eight years, as senator, and as secretary of state, with a law degree and achievements for the public good stretching back to her college days as a demonstrator for civil rights. Like all politicians, she had her own set of problems and prejudices, but no one could say that her deeds were anywhere in the category of Trump's moral meanness and unhinged mendacity. Many of his actions showed that he disliked women, thought of them as less than men, and viewed them as objects useful only for his personal pleasure. Almost every woman who came into his orbit had to submit to his male chauvinism, deeply weakened ego, and ruthless patriarchy. He proved to be a fearful man, and he bluffed his way to the presidency by appealing to latent racist proclivities among the least educated Americans.

There have been and there will always be debates about the true nature of democracy. The idea in Athens, Greece, was that all citizens were equal, although we know that Athens had its own problems. Those who had property were considered the true citizens, and their voices were far more powerful than the voices of those who were without wealth. Rome would continue the process of developing democracy with an eye toward supporting the principle that wealth gave one more freedom. It would be centuries before the founders of the American nation challenged the British Empire with their notion of individual liberty. Each person's house was to be his castle, and there were to be no persons beyond the law. Indeed, the meetings in Philadelphia, Pennsylvania, that established the founding documents—after the demise of the decades (or so)–old Confederacy, which had been set up after the Declaration of Independence—sought to enshrine the principles of a dynamic democracy where human beings would be equal under the law. The Constitution, flawed as it was by the enslavement of Africans, the shunting of the Native Nations, and the invisibility of women in the law, held out the possibility of equality. Indeed, this possibility is what morphed into the hope and optimism felt by those who could neither read nor vote; their sight was insight, and their knowledge of what was in the Constitution was only from hearsay and rumor. On these thin threads dangling from the Constitution, millions of men and women tied their hopes. What my ancestors could not read, they could imagine, and they knew there would come a time when the Constitution would fulfill its promises. I grew up with the feeling that we would eventually be able to agitate for our rights under the law.

Our struggle for human rights, often translated as civil rights, against the legislated segregationist and racist practices of the nation, helped create the platform for numerous other movements for freedom. This is why we say that the long African fight for freedom has been America's true journey of liberation. Freedom, therefore, was defined by our struggle to throw off bondage. In many ways, this was different from the liberty sought by the white settlers protesting taxation without representation. Our struggle was for freedom from enslavement.

Civility can be fleeting given the rhetoric of a lying demagogue. Even individuals who are normally civil toward their fellows discover in the rhetoric of the demagogue an evil path toward community dissension, and often they stride toward society's breakdown thinking that they are operating in their own best interest when in fact they are simply falling into a dangerous trap laid by the demagogue for his own political interest.

The aim of laws is to regulate human activity for the interest of all, but even laws cannot prevent citizens who are full of racial, class, or religious animosity toward their neighbors from listening to the demagogue who seeks to divide people. This is different from dividing people on the basis of arguments against or for a particular policy. One cannot claim to be for democracy while at the same time distorting the meaning of democracy by shaping it in the image of race, religion, or class.

Inherent in democracy, especially when the institutions of a democratic society work, is the ability of the people to throw off the demagogue. This is the promise we have inherited as a nation through the sweat and blood of many movements in the past century, such as the Civil Rights Movement, the Students' Movement, the Women's Movement, the Black Power Movement, and so forth. The clearest assault on irrationality is rationality; the key to unlocking shady operators in mendacious words and actions is confrontation, sharply and often. A demagogue feeds off of the shouts and applause of the crowd like a vulture off of dead meat. In this case, the demagogue throws the dead meat to the audience, and when they respond, he in turn responds to their applause. In reality, both the demagogue who has thrown the wordy meat and those who have received it share in killing any form of rational dialogue. They form one long monologue of self-glorification.

Although the presidency of Trump has ended, I believe that it is necessary to record how we got to this place in American democracy—I mean this place where we are no longer the beacons of hope for the millions who are destitute in the world. How did we get to this place where we are willing to roll back the clock on health care, environmental protection, disease control, and racial integration and diversity? What I have tried to demonstrate using the best angles on data that I can muster is that the resilience of American democracy throughout history has always been able to smother the demagogue.

CHAPTER 1

The Demagogue

As a student during the 1960s, I had a teacher of communication whose name was Friedrich Casmir; we called him simply Fred L.[1] By the time I enrolled in Pepperdine University for my masters in communication, Casmir had already made a name for himself as a teacher and preacher. He had been in Adolf Hitler's Youth Corps and after the defeat of the Nazis had entered Ohio State University and got his PhD. He traveled around the United States giving a talk called from "From the Swastika to the Cross."[2]

It was from Casmir that I learned about the dangers of demagoguery, although I never quite believed at that time that he had completely purged himself of the effects of living in a society where the supreme leader wanted others to see him, as many did, as a demigod with unimpeachable qualities. It would be later, after the Black Power Movement, Casmir's losing campaign to be in the House of Representatives, and many conversations, and because of Casmir's tremendous faith in my career goals that I began to see, and he too began to see, that we could be friends.

---

[1] I was fortunate to have met Casmir during his most productive days at Pepperdine in the 1960s. He was a famous professor on campus who taught the only course in communication on persuasion. His personal knowledge of the tactics of Goebbels during the Nazi regime was exceptional since he had participated in that campaign.
[2] See https://www.facebook.com/events/776196122448656/. This site provides Casmir's lecture.

I saw Leni Riefenstahl's film *Triumph of the Will*, which was considered one of the most powerful propaganda films ever made at that time. The film deeply etched itself into my memory and reappeared in my imagination every time I learned something about the fickleness of rationality. I have given much thought to the willingness of the Germans of the Third Reich to give up their own rationality to fall for the propaganda of the rambunctious and determined cadre of Aryan supremacists who surrounded Hitler.[3] Many of them were ordinary citizens trying to eke out a living in an unstable economy.

Wearing their brown shirts and shouting cruel and terrorist threats at Jews, Roma, and gays, the Nazi votarists, led by extremist thinking and the rhetoric of Adolf Hitler, dominated the airwaves and media attention in Germany. They became Hitler's oratorical barnstormers, who set the nation on fire as it waited for the words of der Fuhrer.

What propelled Hitler to the leadership of Germany? Given the fact that Hitler openly preached anti-Semitism and believed in the superiority of the German people, why would the people see him as a leader? For him, there was nothing wrong with the German society except that it had opened itself up to an "invasion" by non-German people. The idea was to create and maintain a purely German state with people who had German blood.[4] All demagogues like using biology to separate their people from the aliens. Once they have identified the enemy as the other, they are ready to destroy the other.

THE NORMALIZATION OF DEMAGOGUERY

I think that we should remember that Hitler and the Nazi Party lost the election of 1932, but President Paul von Hindenburg appointed him as

---

[3]Erika Wenzel Vora, *The Development of Concept Diffusion Models and Their Application to the Diffusion of the Social Concept of Race*. Buffalo: SUNY–Buffalo, 1978.

[4]Benjamin Carter Hett, *The Death of Democracy: Hitler's Rise to Power and the Downfall of the Weimar Republic*. New York: Holt, 2018. Hett explores how Germany's democracy caved in so quickly, which led to the collapse and transformation of the nation's institutions under the rhetoric and bombast of the Hitlerian extremist con.

chancellor in January 1933. A few months later, in March, the Reichstag passed the Enabling Act of 1933, which sealed Hitler's rise to power. It was a mere ten years since the Munich Beer Hall putsch introduced Hitler's bombastic and racist brand of oratory to the German people.

The demagogue believes that he has a right to rule because he is smarter than other people. In a twisted way, he sees himself not as Plato's philosopher king but as a natural leader because of his supposed higher intelligence. In Trump's case, there is little evidence that he has had a liberal education or a wide understanding of the contemporary world. To attend school or college is different from being educated. Trump neither reads deeply, nor is he willing to be taught by those who do read seriously. He is like a fidgety child who responds only to commands barked by someone who he believes is more powerful than he is.

Hitler was the one speaker from the Nazi Party who could arouse the raw emotions of the crowd repeatedly. Finally, he threatened to resign from the party if his colleagues did not make him the leader. He believed that he was the most gifted and the best suited to be the leader, and consequently the people made him their leader.[5]

Trump's desire for power came forth out of a desire for revenge, something that he had felt most of his life, probably even when his father placed him in military school to "teach" him discipline. No one can tell what really happened in that school. Did the young bully meet other bullies who were bigger and stronger?

It does seem that this experience gave him a deference toward and reverence for those in military positions. He came to love the title "General," and I believe that he would have preferred those around him to see him as a great general. This is why generals such as Michael Flynn, H. R. McMaster, James Mattis, and John Kelly were prominent in his first government.

---

[5]Geoffrey Pridham, *Hitler's Rise to Power: The Nazi Movement in Bavaria 1923–33*. London: Lume Books, 2016. Pridham demonstrates how Hitler came to power in Bavaria and went on to gain national power because he was able to ride the wave of anti-Semitism and bigotry he found in the German people. As the country was led into the abyss by euphoria over the creation of a pure German state, the people lost their freedom and their democracy.

All one has to do is to examine the life and career of the most prominent European demagogue of the twentieth century to get a glimpse of what an American demagogue would look like in the twenty-first century.

I have no evidence that Trump studied the speeches of Hitler, but I have a powerful suspicion that Hitler was a figure he admired in German history, and being impressed by Hitlerian rhetoric may have been a part of his family's attachment to the German martial heritage. Using demagogic language and wild conspiracy theories, Hitler spoke to his political base, people who felt left behind, economically, and culturally, in an effort to "wake them up" to the dangers that the saw were surrounding them.

THE DANGER IN THE OTHER

Trump sees an America that is overrun by immigrants. In his judgment, the nation's southern border is so porous that the country will soon be filled with undocumented aliens. He has been able to give this false picture to his political base in towns where his followers were the last immigrant families, and they only see contemporary immigrants on the television. They have often drunk the lemonade, so to speak, or hung the picture he has given them of immigrants on the walls of their brain.

Der Fuhrer showed his mass audiences in Germany the same broken picture. For Hitler, it was the "yoke of the Jews and communists," and for Trump, it was Muslims, Mexicans, Africans, Asians, and Haitians who were dangerous for the American nation. Hitler's preference for the Aryan and Nordic types can now be seen in Trump's preference for Nordic and Aryan people. He infamously said, "Why can't we have more Norwegians" after he had decried the immigration of Africans and Haitians from "shithole countries."[6]

---

[6]*The Washington Post*, on January 12, 2018, reported that President Trump referred to Haiti and African nations as "shithole countries" during a meeting with a bipartisan group of senators at the White House, as told to NBC News by a Democratic aide briefed on the meeting.

When Trump announced his run for the presidency, he expressed his beliefs about people who were not like him in that speech. He declared,

> When Mexico sends its people, they're not sending their best. They're not sending you. They're not sending you. They're sending people that have lots of problems, and they're bringing those problems with them. They're bringing drugs. They're bringing crime. They're rapists. And some, I assume, are good people.

Straight out of the classical demagogue's playbook, Trump chose another to begin his campaign. His was not a speech of promise, hope, progress, and vision but a dark and stained view of petty politics using the model of the demagogue. Attacking the Mexicans seemed particularly easy and divisive since the Mexican population is set to grow rapidly and Trump's idea was that to tap into the animosity that many whites have against "colored" immigrants would gain voter approval among white populations.

I have yet to hear that Trump is calling for a white empire that would "rule the world for a thousand years," which is the preferred number for demagogues such as Ian Smith of Rhodesia and Hitler of the Nazi regime. In Africa, the last genuine demagogue was not Robert Mugabe but Ian Smith, who made an appeal to the white Rhodesians for a regime that would rule for "a thousand years." Instead, what Trump has done is to rile up a minority of whites who are solidly in his camp, who are against immigrants and would insist that the door be shut on what he has called "chained immigration." What is this *chain migration* but the most humane form of immigration? It is precisely the path taken by many European families who immigrated; they came and later they sent for their mothers, fathers, nieces and nephews, and sometimes their grandparents. Why should this door be closed to contemporary immigrants? Are we sensing something ominous about the nature of Trump's rhetoric? Is the fear of others so prominent in his mind and among his political base that we are seeing evidence of the breakdown of the American ideal?

Whenever you insert the seed of racism in the immigration policy of a nation, especially one that is built with people from other nations, you are creating a dangerous and explosive situation because it pits those identified as citizens against noncitizens, and whites against Mexicans, Africans, and so on.

Sometimes it is useful to have a good American history lesson. But perhaps we should start with a history of world democracies, and we would see clearly that democracies do not die; they are murdered when the people lose sight of the democratic vision. Democracy is a powerful idea, but it is difficult when you have agitators willing to substitute the rule of the rich or the rule of race for the rule of the people. Another reason why reading is important not just for the leaders but also for the masses is because it enhances the ability to make wise decisions. Demagogues insist that people cannot rule themselves without the leadership of the "smart" ones with the "really good genes." In this case, the nation descends swiftly into bitter and sometimes warring factions led by a demagogic tyrant. History teaches us that there is always only one end to that road: the demise of the nation and the end of the tyrant.

Michael Wolff says that Trump had an obsession for firing people—for example, Rod Rosenstein, James Comey, Robert Mueller, Christopher Wray, Jeff Sessions, or whichever person he felt threatened by on a particular day.[7] This fascination with ending the careers of opponents in a crushing way is in the spirit of a tyrant. Of course, he has all of the flaws of a petty leader: a desire for patrimonialism, paranoia, profligacy, populism, and jealousy of previous leaders.

The demagogue constantly goes to his political base for rallies, where emotional energy is always kicked up by being against something or someone. Trump has a depressingly large number of targets, which completely drive his audiences nuts with yells and screams when he mentions their names. His attacks on anyone who appears to threaten the way he perceives himself are always couched as his way of defending not only himself but also his political followers. The rallies of the right are always full of venom; Trump stirs up the basest emotions and then leaves people to see conspiracies everywhere, although they have nothing of substance to which they can point. Mexicans are not criminals, and Africans do not come from "shithole" countries. Stupidity reigns only as long as the truth is not revealed.

---

[7]Michael Wolff, *The Last Word With Lawrence O'Donnell*, MSNBC, January 27, 2018.

THE ONLY SMART ONE

Trump tells his political base that the leaders who came before him were dumb, stupid, and political fools who got swindled by foreign leaders and nations such as China and Mexico, whose leaders were smarter than the American leaders. During his rise to the presidency, Trump attacked all of his opponents and even the progressive actions that had been taken by the presidents before him. He showed his personal angst at Obama's liberal and humanistic legacy and vowed to take down all of the former president's executive actions. In his speeches, he attacked trade agreements, the Iran agreement, the North American Free Trade Agreement, the Pacific-Asian Partnership, the Paris Accords on Climate, and anything that Obama had supported.

"I am really smart," the demagogue says to his emotional followers, who often look at his business dealings as evidence of how smart he really is. But a person who inherited millions and works to maintain those millions, and maybe to increase the amount, is not necessarily demonstrating evidence of intellect but could be demonstrating greed, stealth, theft, and bluster. Money cannot be equated with wisdom or intellect. The Odu Ifa says that if you have money but do not have character, the money does not belong to you.

Like most bullies, Trump is a fake. However, it is his insecurity based on the fact that he is not as smart as those who read rather than his boasting that propels him into an association with demagoguery. Why would an American president want to ask the military to provide him with a martial parade to show off America's weapons? Have we come to the end of the American era? How did a demagogue, interested in his own glory, not that of his country, ever rise in a democracy? These questions sit at the door to understanding the assertion of the demagogue to gather power to himself.

THE MICRO-AGGRESSIONS OF WEAKNESS

Ana Monteiro Ferreira, the author of *The Demise of the Inhuman*, claims that micro-aggressions are the tools of the arrogant. In recent years, we have not seen any politician with as many weapons of micro-aggression in his arsenal as Trump.[8] He not only has those weapons, but he is also quick to draw them against any politician who might win glory from the masses. His dislike for the venerable John McCain and Mitt Romney may have come from his desire to be seen as the savior of the Republican Party.

Trump's adoption of the ultra-right was his quickest path to political victory because the ultra-right built populism on the basis of micro-aggressions against others. Trump saw the movement as needing a strong leader around whom all of the right could coalesce. Although Trump had lived a life that betrayed the values that the Evangelical Christians and the white nationalists said they believed in, he was able to convince them that he was, in effect, like them. Although Trump was a billionaire and many of his followers were mostly the working poor and actually poor, they felt that he would protect and support their interests. Demagogues always speak as though they are one with the people—that they have common interests and rely on the people to give them direction. A demagogue therefore is not to be confused with a tyrant, although there are similarities. Trump appears to want to act like a tyrant. He muses why he cannot order "his guys" to carry out his commands. He wants "his" people to do as he says even if it is not in the interest of the nation. He wants his cabinet minister to "serve" him because he identifies himself as the nation. Demagogues can morph into tyrants if they are allowed to do so by weakening the democratic institutions.

OF DEMAGOGUES AND TYRANTS

Tyrants have a long history in Europe and throughout the world. Tyrants are rulers who seize power unconstitutionally or who are thrust into leadership by inheritance but then brutalize their people as if they are the only voice that can or should be heard. The best known of these types of rulers were Cypselus at Corinth and Orthagoras at Sicyon from about 650 BCE. Of course, the tyrant would continue to appear in societies. Thus, in Athens, the title of tyrant was first given to Peisistratos,

---

[8]Ana Monteiro-Ferreira, *The Demise of the Inhuman*. Albany: SUNY Press, 2013.

ironically a relative of the famous lawgiver Solon. In 546, he succeeded in making himself a tyrant after two unsuccessful attempts. Later, Lysander imposed 30 tyrants on the Athenian population after the capitulation to Sparta at the end of the Peloponnesian War in 404 BC (Black Caucus). These men were dictators with no barriers and no constraints to prevent them from doing harm and brutalizing the public to keep order.

There is always danger when people give up their rational abilities to follow a "smart" leader. As African Americans, we fought for the right to express our political preferences and name our own leaders who would ensure that our interests would be protected. If the interests are not even on the table, one cannot be respected.

THE MEDIA AND DEMOCRACY

The attack on the demagogue begins with relentless facts. As Michelle Obama said about Trump, he did not understand that America was a "rebuke of tyranny." But we know that the source of demagogic power is ignorance. One way to challenge demagogues is to shine the light of knowledge on their rhetoric. Once a people have elected a demagogue, they cannot go back and ask him to read American history.

Those who would destroy democracy first seek to control the means of information. How do you inform the people? What do you know, and where do you get the information? A fundamental part of the process of the destruction of democracy is the rewriting of history. Thus, it is not only the present that must be distorted but also the past. The person who does not know the past will inevitably twist the present to shape the future.

While traveling outside the United States, I normally do not listen to any news from the United States; I listen to the local news. Inside the United States, one lives in a bubble of news that surrounds Trump. If it is on Fox, it is pro-Trump; on most other networks, it is critical of the demagoguery, although it seeks to be balanced, which, of course, is a false concept. Either something is true and correct, or it is not. Can you imagine a world where Fox News is your only news outlet? You would be totally ignorant, misinformed, hyperactive, and believing that the political reality is what you hear and see, which is often nothing but a maze of worthless conspiracy theories. This is the territory of the demagogue. It is as though someone had gathered all of the conspiracy theorists in one place, and they repeat the same lines over and over again like parrots in a word cage.

A powerful and careful media is essential in a democracy. These people need to write commentaries, inform one another about what is going on with the elected leaders, and refresh their own wells of information by reading, debating with respect, and writing with logic. The reason it was once said that democracy is based strictly on talk is because at one point of time, people believed that whatever comes out of your mouth should be deeply reflected on before you speak. The Native Peoples believed that once you have spoken, you wait for a minute or two to allow your words to sink in so that if you need to correct them before they are final, you can do so. There is a tendency among demagogues to believe that fast talking is a characteristic of intelligence, when it is actually more likely the characteristic of lightweight thinking about substantive issues.

Every communication scholar and every rhetorician know that a demagogue is a person who aspires to attain and maintain power by appealing to the base desires, prejudices, and fears of the public. A demagogue does not favor rational discourse and argument but rather seeks to control the actions and opinions of people by appealing to their worst instincts.

Finding out what people fear through opinion polls or surveys or a natural ability to listen to others who preach emotional rhetoric, such as news commentators, can give the demagogue ammunition for control. If you listen to commentators telling you how many foreigners are taking jobs away from your community, you may be inclined to listen to a demagogue who blames foreigners instead of making a solid analysis based on economics. In fact, some people who have never encountered an international person will claim that they are unable to find jobs because of international people. "You do not have to see them to fear them" becomes the maxim.

WHAT IS DEMAGOGUERY?

I believe that the demagogue is especially attuned to the psychology of the masses for his own benefit.

There are some classic definitions of a demagogue, and Reinhard Luthin was quite succinct when he defined a demagogue in this way:

> A politician skilled in oratory, flattery, and invective; evasive in discussing vital issues; promising everything to everybody; appealing to the passions rather than the reason of the public; and arousing racial, religious, and class prejudices—a man whose lust for power without recourse to principle leads him to seek to become a master of the masses. He has for centuries practiced his profession of "man of the people."[9]

Here it is: the person who has knowledge about flattery and is able to say with ease that someone is the greatest, most intelligent, finest, most gifted, or most beautiful but never as great as the demagogue himself. Flattery is a coin of the demagogue. But so is invective a coin against those considered to be enemies or just plain opponents of the demagogue.

The word "demagogue" is derived from the Greek δημαγωγός, which carries with it the idea of a leader of a mob, population, or organization. One of the great thinkers on this issue was Charles Wyatt Lomas, who taught at the University of California, Los Angeles, and wrote a book called *The Agitator in American Society* in 1968. Lomas studied a group of American political and social leaders and concluded that demagogues are most likely rabble-rousing speakers who can appeal to the prejudices of the masses in such a way that they identify their interests with those of the demagogue. However, he was clear that an agitator is not necessarily a demagogue but rather one who want to incite the people, especially those with grievances, to protest to the powerful to change a law, rule, or condition. The agitator, therefore, is an activist on behalf of others.

On the other hand, the rhetorical power of a demagogue rests in the idea that all established protocols are against the people and must be overturned. The demagogue promises to do what others cannot do and would not do. As a result, the demagogue seeks to overturn protocols that he did not set up, destroy ordinary customs of decent conduct, disestablish the agencies, corrupt the regulatory bodies, and promise something entirely new and better. Only on rare occasions will a demagogue bring

---

[9]Reinhard H. Luthin, *American Demagogues*. Boston, MA: Beacon Press, 1954, p. 3.

into existence anything better. If he promises better health care, you will get nothing better. If he promises that you will get tired of winning, you will see only losses. The point of the demagogue is to satisfy his own ego.

Using the most salient mark of the rhetorical process, that is, persuasion, the demagogue understands that human beings have unlearned drives that can be manipulated toward narcissistic, nationalistic, and racist ends. Tapping into these drives can lead to certain negative behaviors. An effective orator or rhetor deals with rational discourse in an effort to persuade through argument. Hence, persuasion can be examined for its emotional, rational, and ethical content.

Demagoguery is coexistent with democracy itself, but it is never necessary for democracy. In many ways, the political process that accompanies democracy is extremely vulnerable to the demagogue. Since the fundamental power of a democracy is supposed to be the people and not a court, or a legislature, or even the rich oligarchs who might control the mighty technological empire of a nation, the demagogue can exploit the emotions of the people to gain access to democratic power. One might say that demagoguery hides in the corners of democracy. It is possible for people to give power to bullies who appeal to the lowest common denominator of a large part of society. One can never underestimate the desire of the masses to identify with those they consider powerful. Trump knows that celebrity and wealth give him much more latitude to act as he does.

All demagogues know that the best way to appeal to people is to say that they are special, different in substance and nature from other people, and that they can be the salvation of a society in trouble if they take immediate action, such as electing the demagogue to power. The demagogue often advocates an immediate and hardline agenda to show that he means business. In effect, the demagogue proposes something that a rational human being would question.

Enter Donald Trump, the latest American to use demagoguery to win power!

Trump is a billionaire, but he convinced a sufficient number of poor whites to vote for him because he understood their inner fears, their political desire to be exceptional, perhaps to feel superior to others. Consequently, Trump became a white nationalist leader who became the president of the United States with almost no African American votes and only a few Latin American votes.

There are two aspects to Trump's wealth, the foundation for his political rise: (1) he is a *real estate mogul* and (2) he was a *prominent television personality*. By combining money with celebrity, Trump was able to rise above and to climb over all his political opponents.

Many people knew him from his real estate business because he built buildings and branded them with his name. These projects were hotels, golf courses, casinos, and office buildings. Trump branded and licensed his name to be used in managing this financial empire.

Trump also maximized his celebrity when he became a political demagogue by hosting *The Apprentice*, a television reality show, from 2003 to 2015. He also coauthored the book *The Art of the Deal*. A businessperson with a hard-nosed reputation for aggressive competition even if it meant the obliteration of the competitor, Trump managed to control two pageants, Miss Universe, and Miss USA, for nearly twenty years. It is safe to say from comments made by some of the contestants that he saw the pageants as his personal sexual playground. Nothing he desired was ever off the shelf, and he felt that denial by a woman was not possible, particularly because he was a celebrity and wealthy. *Forbes* magazine called him the 544th richest person in the world with nearly 3.5 billion dollars, far less than some had thought initially.

Given the fact that he used his demagoguery to defeat 16 Republican opponents to become the party's nominee for president, Trump's antics, and perhaps those of the Russians, increased his boldness in upping the demagoguery against Hillary Clinton. The official line has been that the Russians had no impact on the election. This is not credible because I personally know people who either did not vote or voted against Clinton after ingesting the bitterness spewed out by the Russians; and of course, Trump's willingness to amplify these negative messages showed his lack of restraint.

Trump had no well-defined theories about politics except to appeal to the masses as an American protectionist, populist, and white nationalist. His followers immediately understood that he was someone who would ride with them toward a much more radically conservative country.

Because of his wealth and celebrity, his populist views, often expressed with flair, managed to get immense free publicity and circulation. Running against Clinton, a formidable candidate with the best credentials of anyone who has run for the office, Trump used all of his political energy to defeat the progressive wing of American politics. Not only did Trump become the wealthiest and oldest person to assume the office, but he also became the most outspokenly narcissistic and Nationalist president in a century.

THE APPEAL OF SEPARATION FOR THE DEMAGOGUE

The African American community found him to be tone-deaf about the multicultural, pluralistic, and progressive pitch of the American nation. Of course, he had demonstrated his inability to accept African American leadership in his attack on Obama. Trump's leadership of the Birther Movement sealed his toxic rhetoric and character in history and associated him with racial bigotry. He would prove to be a religious bigot as well. Like a demagogue, he would always claim that he was the least racist and bigoted person, all the while demonstrating his dislike of Mexicans, Muslims, and people from Africa.

Gathering an unusual conglomeration of anti-Muslim, anti-Semitic, anti-African, and homophobic patriarchs deeply rooted in the Evangelical Christian faith, Trump went on his journey to steal the American democracy by employing the most vicious rhetoric seen in any recent presidential campaign. Neither Barry Goldwater nor George Wallace was ever accused of being so blatantly antidemocratic in their rhetoric. They were certainly not progressive, but they used symbolism, sentimental terminology, *double entendre*, and suggestion to persuade their audiences.

A demagogue seeks and gains power by creating a group of people who believe that he is a deliverer because he states that he is the only one who can make things happen. He plays on the passions of the less educated and the poorer classes, who are willing to give their trust to a self-promoting demagogue. He can claim that he is smarter, tougher, and wealthier than anyone else. No one can compare with him; he is supreme in his mind and therefore seeks to dominate all others.

Sycophants gravitate toward demagogues in a waltz of mutual necessity. By demanding that those who "believe" in him give one hundred percent of their trust to him, the demagogue is able to use and abuse the sycophant at will. On the other hand, the sycophant gains by being close to power. In some cases, as with Michael Cohen, Trump's erstwhile lawyer, close associates can try to capitalize on their access to the demagogue.

The American novelist, as early as 1838, identified four basic characteristics of demagogues:[10]

1. They fashion themselves as a man or woman of the common people opposed to elites.
2. Their politics depends on a visceral connection with the people beyond ordinary political popularity.
3. They manipulate this connection, and the raging popularity it affords, for their own benefit and ambition.
4. They threaten to and, in some cases, go ahead and outright break the established rules of conduct, institutions, and even the law.

Americans know Cooper as the first major American novelist, but this New Jersey–born writer, the author of *The Pioneers* (1823), *The Last of the Mohicans* (1826), *The Prairie* (1827), *The Pathfinder* (1840), and *The Deerslayer* (1841), was also a keen observer of history and an astute student of human behavior.

However, most authorities believe that it was in his novel *The Bravo* (1831) that he explored the political corruption that he had seen and experienced when he traveled in Europe. Tyranny and political conspiracies created a patched fabric of bitterness that caused the masses to revolt against the oligarchy. I believe that Cooper became a leading voice against demagoguery because he did not want his own nation to fall into the trap of endless struggles against demagogues and tyrants that he had witnessed during his travels in Europe. Of course, the United States was not immune from political intrigue, as the presidency of Andrew Jackson,

---

[10]https://en.wikipedia.org/wiki/James_Fenimore_Cooper.

known as the "Indian Fighter," also stirred the emotions of the masses. He was not, however, the model for Trump, although Trump hung Jackson's picture in the Oval Office. Not only was Jackson a racist slave owner, but he also oversaw the "Trail of Tears" that displaced thousands of Native Americans in order to give their lands to whites, who made that land the basis of their wealth. Jackson sought a white republic for white people. Black people are not amused by Trump's whistles to the most reactionary communities in the country. Demagogues dwell in the valley of difference; they do not see the possibilities in unity. One has only to see Obama's rhetoric of "no red states and no blue states, only the United States of America" to realize the dumbing down found in Trump's jingoistic appeals to populism.

CHAPTER 2

The Fear of Fear

The demagogue trades in fear, but fear has little currency in the face of knowledge. We often think that this fear trade is what describes Donald Trump's political rhetoric, but obviously it has always been a part of his deal: Scare the *other* person. In the summer of 1988, when he received an honorary doctorate from Lehigh University, Trump declared that America was losing out to other nations because we did not have strong leaders. This derisive and divisive personality trait seems to have been with him most of his adult life. His entire persona is to name those he likes and dismiss those he dislikes, especially stirring up the emotions of the lower classes, one among whom he is not, against the elites, representing his own economic class. What he trades in is the fear that is in the hearts of many of the undereducated and uneducated who are left behind and of economically depressed whites. There is the shock that they carry when they see the increase in immigrants, documented and undocumented; there is also the disdain they feel when Blacks, once enslaved in this land, are often able to manage with far less than whites. Trump understands these fears, and he knows precisely how to play on them as a good populist. Whatever his political base populations are against, he is against. What they are for, he is also for—until he changes his mind.

I surmise that the demagogue's tactic is to ensure that he will have at least one supporter, although no one is really secure standing close to him. Not only is agreeing with him or supporting him like "jello," as Senator

Chuck Schumer once said about negotiating with Trump, but it is like soup. You cannot get in the pot with him without becoming dirty; that is the way Trump plots his life, seeking to overshadow all events and every other person.

But creating fear is not a philosophy or a political platform; it is a political tactic. Shaka ka Sengakhona, the great warrior king of the Zulus, Shaka ka Sengakhona, is reputed to have said, "If you show your enemies and your friends your capacity to cause fear, you will gain in immediate popularity." I sometimes think that this is the demagogue's greatest danger to any nation—that is, the ability to inflict punishment and assume that it will not return to you or your country.

Why did Trump ask the military to drop the mother of all bombs on Afghanistan when he took office? Dropping a 22,000-pound bomb, the MOAB (the GBU-43/B Massive Ordnance Air Blast), has been compared by the Pentagon to dropping a small nuclear bomb. It is not even possible to drop it from a warplane as it is so large; it has to be rolled out of the back of a cargo plane and outfitted with a parachute. Trump, I believe, wanted to show that he was willing to use the largest conventional bomb in America's arsenal to bring about psychological fear[1] Of course, other demagogues are capable as well of demonstrating such wanton designs on human populations. So there is an immediate political bump, perhaps in fear of the demagogue who is irrational enough to kill hundreds of people without remorse. Indeed, remorse is replaced by recrimination in the demagogue's playbook.

Such immediate response is no indication that a leader can control the longevity of fear. People can be fearful at one moment and not at another. Through study and analysis, one can reduce the level of fear or understand what the causes are of fear. This emotion is nothing more than our anticipation that something or someone will cause us danger, harm, or hurt. Yet we can be in control of our emotions much more than those who preach violence against others or their followers simply because we understand our own actions. If I am peaceful or nonviolent

---

[1]Robin Wright, "Trump Drops the Mother of All Bombs on Afghanistan," *New Yorker*, April 14, 2017.

in my actions, I do not expect violence in return; yet I am certainly wise enough to know that it is possible that I may be attacked, just as the peaceful Civil Rights marchers were beaten at the Edmund Winston Pettus Bridge over the Alabama River at Selma, Alabama, on Bloody Sunday, March 7, 1965.

Looking at the plethora of cult leaders who have convinced people to follow them, one quickly understands the power of fear. The true believer is a person who has abandoned rationality. This means that you have accepted the words of fear that come from the demagogue without question. Trump appeals to three levels of fear in his followers: *economic*, *existential*, and *criminal*.

During his initial speech for his political campaign for the presidency, Trump laid out what the public had to fear. On June 16, 2015, these are some of the ideas that Trump stated in stark terms:

Economics

"When do we beat Mexico at the border? They're laughing at us, at our stupidity. And now they are beating us economically. They are not our friends, believe me. But they're killing us economically."

"That's right. A lot of people up there can't get jobs. They can't get jobs because there are no jobs, because China has our jobs and Mexico has our jobs. They all have jobs."

Existential

"Our enemies are getting stronger and stronger by the way, and we as a country are getting weaker. Even our nuclear arsenal doesn't work."

Criminality

"When Mexico sends its people, they're not sending their best. They're not sending you. They're not sending you. They're sending people that have lots of problems, and they're bringing those problems with us. *They're bringing drugs. They're bringing crime. They're rapists.* And some, I assume, are good people."

Trump's denouement was announced in these words: "Now, our country needs, our country needs a truly great leader, and we need a truly great leader now. We need a leader that wrote *The Art of the Deal*." This is classic demagoguery of the first order. No one can do this job, he claims, but himself.

By way of contrast, when Senator Obama announced his candidacy for the presidency in 2007, he declared,

> We all made this journey for a reason. It's humbling, but in my heart, I know you didn't come here just for me; you came here because you believe in what this country can be. In the face of war, you believe there can be peace. In the face of despair, you believe there can be hope. In the face of a politics that's shut you out, that's told you to settle, that's divided us for too long, you believe we can be one people, reaching for what's possible, building that more perfect union.

Furthermore, his denouement closed out the announcement with this humble call for togetherness:

> And if you will join me in this improbable quest, if you feel destiny calling and see, as I see, a future of endless possibility stretching before us, if you sense, as I sense, that the time is now to shake off our slumber and slough off our fear and make good on the debt we owe past and future generations, then I'm ready to take up the cause and march with you and work with you. Together, starting today, let us finish the work that needs to be done and usher in a new birth of freedom on this earth.

The difference in speech is clear, and one feels the inspiration, the hope, and the desire to lift all Americans in the deeply virtuous ideas presented in Obama's speech. In Obama's tone and words, there are no demons, no devils, and no enemies, only Americans with myriad challenges.

Democracy demands skepticism. A certain amount of doubt or a skeptical attitude will create a more viable democracy. The aim of some politicians in a democracy is to gain your vote, not to tell you the truth. Of course, we are fortunate that there has been a long tradition of politicians trying to satisfy their constituents without the use of fear. Others, such as demagogues, keep the people anxious, fearful of one another, and looking for enemies everywhere. At a moment when many Americans felt fear during the Second Great International War, President Franklin Roosevelt declared, "We have nothing to fear but fear itself!"

The demagogue loves fear because he is a bully. He enjoys seeing others tremble when they see him. He speaks to those who are weak as if he is the only savior for them. And weak people are always the ones who look toward the demagogue, who declares how tough he is and how willing he is to speak on their behalf. We have watched as Trump used every device in the process of seducing the masses with his reality show celebrity.

Trump seems willing to sacrifice everyone and everything with his boasting about what should happen to his opponents. One does not see generosity in the demagogue; one only sees the outlines of a scared little boy who has better clothes, more money, and more material things than his peers but does not have *soul*, that ability to feel for the human condition in such a way as to demonstrate true empathy. Rather, he uses the fears of his audiences for self-adulation and political advantage. There is something sinister about a person who shares almost nothing with those who follow him (and knows it) yet uses his explanations for their condition as a way to dominate their thinking.

Trump is not a $29,000 a year man; he probably makes that amount of money in a few minutes if his reported wealth is what is claimed. Trump's followers are not his peers when it comes to membership in his clubs; it would take hundreds of them to find the money to pay the membership fees. Trump's health care is not the same for those who follow him. Demagogues cultivate reactionary followers who will fall for his lines against other people, but they do not raise the level of reasoning, purpose, or American unity. Therefore, their use of fear as a rhetorical tactic is venal.

In Trump's case it is not his wealth that is troubling but his attempt to claim that he is the champion of the poor whites that makes his rhetoric dangerous. It is false, fake, and artificial because it is an empty artifice used to manipulate the masses. He has shown an ability to use his mad-dog visage and countenance to trample on all the good other people achieve. He seeks adherents who will not question his judgment, tactics, or policies.

Trump did everything to criminalize those who did not support him during the election campaign of 2015. He attacked the Republicans who ran against him as weak, unintelligent, lazy, and low energy, thus making them different from himself because he saw himself as intelligent and energetic. Trump viewed himself as the most perfect candidate to ever run for the presidency. This was a theme he would continue to use during his first year in office as president.

Perhaps no losing political opponent has ever been assaulted as Hillary Clinton was during the campaign. During the time of the campaign, Trump attacked Hillary Clinton with shouts of "Lock her up!" This was not enough; he also demeaned her character and spoke pejoratively about her health.

Trump had a particular animus it seemed toward African Americans. This may have been due to the discrimination charges filed decades ago by the National Urban League against Trump's properties. In February 2017, the FBI released nearly 400 pages of its investigation into Trump's discriminatory housing practices as far back as the 1970s.[2] Josh Gerstein wrote,

> In October 1973, the Civil Rights Division filed a lawsuit against Trump Management Company, Donald Trump, and his father Fred Trump, alleging that African Americans and Puerto Ricans were systematically excluded from apartments. The Trumps responded with a $100 million countersuit accusing the government of defamation.

The case was eventually settled in 1975 with the stipulation that Trump institute "a series of safeguards to make sure apartments were rented without regard to race, color, religion, sex, or national origin."[3] Of course, by then Trump had established a pattern related to African Americans. When on April 19, 1989, a young white woman, Trisha Melli, was assaulted, raped, and sodomized, the tragedy infuriated the city of New York. The investment banker had been jogging in Central Park when she was attacked, and she remained in a coma for twelve days. Four Black youth had been apprehended on the night of the attack. The investigators discovered that none of the boys' DNA matched with what had been discovered on the victim. Yet the public outcry led by politicians, and

---

[2]Josh Gerstein, *Politico*, February 15, 2017.
[3]ibid.

noticeably by real estate builder Trump, was for the blood of the young
Black men. Within days, Trump took out a full-page ad costing nearly
$100,000 in four newspapers calling for the return of the death penalty.
He said, "Muggers and murderers should be forced to suffer, and when
they kill, they should be executed for their crimes." The young men were
convicted and given sentences ranging from five to fifteen years in prison.

Yet even when in 2002 a serial rapist, Matias Reyes, whose DNA
matched that found on the victim was arrested and confessed to the
crime, Trump refused to back away from his earlier vile claim. In fact, he
doubled down after Reyes was convicted of the crime, saying the four
young Black men were guilty because they had told the police they did it.
Investigators found that the young men had been coerced into confessing
to a crime they did not commit. Trump refused to apologize, saying later
to CNN, "They admitted they were guilty." Still not convinced of the
innocence of the young men, Trump continued, "The police doing the
original investigation say they were guilty. The fact that that case was
settled with so much evidence against them is outrageous." What was
outrageous was Trump's irrational response to the innocence of these
young Black men. It is not as if he had not ever heard of false confessions,
where a disproportionate number of Black men are coerced into confessing to crimes they did not commit by the police. In a more recent example
of his animus, Trump told National Football League owners that they
had to come down harder on the players who expressed their dismay that
the nation did not rise up against police brutality. In other words, Trump
had no sympathy for the thousands of young Black men who are brutal-
ized every day; he acted as if he did not know that the protest was not
against the flag but against police brutality. Colin Kaepernick had started
the protest as a nonviolent response to the litany of murders of Black
men on the streets of America by the police. Trump's reaction was to
weaponize patriotism and to suggest that the young men were doing
something un-American, when what they did by kneeling was ultra-
American. Did Trump side with the victims of brutality, and did he show
empathy toward the players? No, he ranted,

> Wouldn't you love to see one of these NFL owners, when somebody dis-
> respects our flag, to say, "Get that son of a bitch off the field right now.
> Out. He's fired. He's fired!" You know, some owner is going to do that.

He's going to say, "That guy that disrespects our flag, he's fired." And that owner, they don't know it. They don't know it. They'll be the most popular people, for a week. They'll be the most popular people in this country.[4]

A demagogue finds pleasure in recriminations and spurious arguments; it works him up and allows him to express himself in the angriest of tones. Catharsis is the idea that people can find relief from repressed emotions if they discover someone who can show them that it is alright to hate, to enjoy the suffering of others, and to do harm. Trump knows how to use negative images and outlandish ideas to evoke these repressed emotions.

GENETIC SUPERIORITY

Seeking comfort in the belief that one is smarter, more intelligent, or more capable than others is a luxury demagogues love to own, whether it is false or true. Trump starts with the classic identification mark of the traditional racist—claiming that his blood is "good stuff." Trump boasts of his German blood, not realizing that there is no such entity. In fact, the German people are similar to other Europeans since according to scientists the ancient migration routes have been mixed for thousands of years. We know that the vast majority of Europeans, including Germans, descended from three major migrations during the past fifteen thousand years. The origin of all *Homo sapiens* can be traced back to the mother continent, Africa. Migrants have a history of mingling with other people in a sort of remix of cultures.

So where does Trump's pride in "German blood" come from if not from his identification with German culture? Even if he knew German history, he would now know that Germany has expressed itself over the past sixty or more years as a nation of *wilkommenkultur*. Trump is not interested in this progressive and inclusive Germany since he wants something that makes him different from other human beings.

---

[4]Aric Jenkins, "Donald Trump's Speech to the NFL on National Anthem Protests," *Time Magazine*, September 25, 2017.

Trump does not talk only of blood, he talks also of genetics, claiming that he has genetic superiority. In a moment of unscientific insanity, he said,

> All men are created equal—that's not true. When you connect two race-horses, you usually end up with a fast horse. The secretariat doesn't produce slow horses. I have a certain gene. I'm a gene believer. Do you believe in the gene thing? I mean I do. I have great genes and all that stuff, which I'm a believer in.[5]

Trump believes in the racehorse theory. Even more, he believes that some people cannot produce "fast" offspring. He is a racist at his core. This is why he really fears the influx of people from non–northern European nations. The browning of the American population has been going on since the turn of the past century, and Trump sees himself as the doorstopper for unfettered immigration. He has the same old odd understanding of "nation" as other racists.

Nations are not static; the United States is not today what it was a hundred years ago, and it is not today what it will be a hundred years from now. I do not fear that one day the nation will be primarily Spanish or Chinese speaking. What a patriot wishes for is the maintenance of good values, common sense, and self-affirming and dignity-producing ideals. In the American context, a nation is not defined as "blood and soil" but by unifying experiences and a collective purpose.

One of the most terrifying attributes of Trump is that he "demagogues" anything and every idea, placing himself at the center of all discourses. As we have seen, in terms of intellectual ability, he thinks more highly of himself than he ought. Consequently, his language is reprehensible for its self-centeredness and egotism. Anyone who talks excessively about his own importance because of an undue sense of self-regard might be considered an egomaniac.

---

[5]Caroline Mortimer, "Donald Trump Believes He Has Superior Genes," *Independent*, September 30, 2016.

Trump said on CNN,

> Well, I think I was born with a drive for success. I was born with a certain intellect. The fact is you have to be born and be blessed with something up there. God helped me by giving me a certain brain. It's *this*, it's not my salesmanship. *This*—you know what that is? I have an Ivy League education.

He spent his last undergraduate year at Wharton, the business school of the University of Pennsylvania. "I have like a very high aptitude," Trump tapped his head, as an adolescent might do to indicate intelligence.

Trump announces his beliefs, as all demagogues do, because he knows that there are certain people who will share these beliefs. Some will defend his comments as true even though they do not like the fact that the demagogue expresses himself so clearly. They give him a pass because he is bold enough to express their prejudices. Thus, following his race-horse theory, Trump says over and over again something like this:

> You're born a fighter, and I've seen a lot of people who want to fight but can't. Some people cannot genetically handle pressure. I always said that winning is somewhat, maybe, innate. Maybe it's just something you have; you have the winning gene. Frankly it would be wonderful if you could develop it, but I'm not so sure you can. You know I'm proud to have that German blood, there's no question about it. Great stuff.[6]

The demagogue is a frightful person. He operates from a sense of inferiority, and the expression is that of a bully because he wants to convince himself that he is superior. This is fear, pure and simple.

Trump says, "Winning is innate." His many followers, some of who are undereducated believers in white supremacy, came to the same conclusion as Trump. They believe that to win you have to have a superior genetic gift, something given to whites at a higher distribution rate than to any other human group.

---

[6]Marina Fang and J. M. Rieger, "This May Be the Most Horrible Thing That Donald Trump Believes," *Huffpost*, September 28, 2016. https://www.huffpost.com/entry/donald-trump-eugenics_n_57ec4cc2e4b024a52d2cc7f9

Trump believes that he was born with special brain power that makes him good at English, at handling pressure, and at winning. The fact that there are hardline votarists who will not abandon him even if he went to Fifth Avenue in New York and shot someone, as he shockingly said in a political rally, is the essence of fear.

Most demagogues create their own reality. Actually, if they lived in an authentic environment where they were conscious of others, they would see that all around them are examples of "really smart" people who do not have illusions and who come from every ethnic group. The attacks on Mexicans, Africans, Arabs, and anyone who is not Nordic or Aryan means that Trump is a racist. Why would he not want for others what he wanted for whites?

Only the Native Americans are not children of the ships. This is why it makes no sense for politicians to try to demagogue immigration. That is, if you understand the origin of the nation as the United States of America, you know that it has nothing to do with "blood and soil" since the over-whelming majority of the people who call themselves Americans came from other continents. But there are two elements in American society that have been exposed in Trump's America. The first is the fear of strangers, and the second is the doctrine of the superiority of whiteness. Of course, the first strangers to America were whites who landed on the shores of America and were greeted overall with hospitality as far as we know until the Europeans sought to impose their values, culture, and ideas on the land of the Native Americans. This was the beginning of the conflict. Jack Weatherford wrote a book called *Indian Givers: How the Indians of the Americas Transformed the World*, in which he argued that most Americans know next to nothing about the Native peoples.[7]

In fact, Weatherford argued that the concepts of egalitarian democracy and liberty were already in the Native American's vocabulary for governance before the encounter with Europe. These concepts are not derived from Greco-Roman or French culture; they came into being because of Native American ideology and were interpreted and translated into European language and culture.[8]

---

[7]Jack Weatherford, *Indian Givers: How the Indians of the Americas Transformed the World*. New York, NY: Ballantine, 1988.

[8]ibid., p, 128.

Weatherford's work traces many of the early "American" ideals to the examples found in the Mohawk, Algonquin, and Cherokee Nations. Benjamin Franklin engaged in conversations with Native American thinkers and found some of the best forms of government among the Native peoples. *E pluribus unum*, the Latin expression for "Out of many, one," did not mean that out of many nations or people there should be one but rather that out of 13 states there should be one nation. The idea came directly from the Mohawk Confederation.

Trump brings an ominous echo of Hitlerian 1920 and 1930s rhetoric to contemporary American politics. Few want to discuss the elements of Hitler's memes in the words of Trump, but we ignore these seeds to our later peril. If Trump is normalized, his rhetoric will become the easy model for other would-be demagogues who will ride the terrifying wave of blatant white nationalism parading as American exceptionalism to the corrupted shore of political chaos. We cannot be ostriches with heads in the sand; we must be attuned to the virulent elements of racism in the society.

In *Mein Kampf*, Hitler writes,

> Blood mixture and the resultant drop in the racial level is the sole cause of the dying out of old cultures; for men do not perish as a result of lost wars, but by the loss of that force of resistance which is contained only in pure blood. All who are not of good race in this world are chaff. And all occurrences in world history are only expression of the races' instinct for self-preservation. What we must fight for is to safeguard the existence and reproduction of our race and our people, the sustenance of our children and the purity of our blood, the freedom and independence of the fatherland, so that our people may mature for the fulfillment of the mission allotted it by the creator of the universe. Those who are physically and mentally unhealthy and unworthy must not perpetuate their suffering in the body of their children.[9]

The existential fear as Trump sees it is that America is losing its whiteness. What is wrong with Mexicans, Haitians, and Africans immigrating to America except the irrational, insane, and unscientific fear of other people? In Trump's book, those marching to the chant of "blood and

---

[9]Adolf Hitler, *Mein Kampf*. Boston, MA: Houghton Mifflin, 1943, pp. 290–293.

soil" are the true representatives of his America First. Of course, all Norwegians are excepted because they are acceptable. They have the right blood, and there is no *rassenschande* ("racial crime") in mixing with Norwegians.

What must the demagogue convince the people to fear? In Hitler's case, it was the Jewish people, the intellectuals, and the media that they did not control. The Nazis used every controlled media, especially the filmmakers of the time, to propagate the ideas that the male Jew was a sexual predator, Jews were like rats, and the way Jews killed animals for kosher was distasteful. Films such as *The Eternal Jew* were meant to remind Germans that they had to work for a society of pure German blood.

As it was in Germany, so it was to be in Trump's rise to power in the United States; the drumbeat for an American exceptionalism that carried with it racist and religious overtones would become the favorite coin of the demagogue.

White nationalists, racist groups, and right-wing protesters converged on Charlottesville, Virginia, on August 11–12, 2017, using a Nazi rallying cry. Videos showed that some of the protesters shouted, "Blood and soil," a phrase invoking the Nazi philosophy of *Blut und Boden*. This was the Nazi ideology that stressed ethnic identity and nationalism based on blood descent and territory. The German farmers and peasants celebrated this idea as a virtue for their nationalism.

Of course, in the United States, the only people who are considered indigenous to this land are the Native Americans, not the immigrants from Africa, Asia, or Europe. Regardless of the historical facts, the group that gathered to protest Charlottesville's plan to remove relics of its Confederate past, such as a statue of Confederate General Robert E. Lee, was bent on a torchlight march. The group clashed with counter protesters who promoted calls for "respect, freedom, and unity." The counterprotesters also swamped the reactionaries with a multicultural and multiracial, progressive group of marchers, who confronted the Nazis and white nationalists with a call for national unity without symbols of hatred or false ideologies glorifying slavery. This portends the possibility of a society that will overcome fear and the manipulations of the demagogue.

CHAPTER 3
The Democratic Ideal

Representative Adam Schiff, California Democrat, a ranking member of the House Intelligence Committee, said at the University of Pennsylvania on February 1, 2018, that President Donald Trump was "not a champion of democracy."

We all learned in high school or college that Athenian democracy first appeared in the fifth century BCE in the Greek city-state of Athens.[1] It extended to the area surrounding the city, called Attica. This was the first identified democracy in the Western world. It has a long and idealized history.

Demagogues have always challenged democracy; but the system has demonstrated its resilience, although it has been vulnerable to fractures caused by those who seek to destroy its effectiveness.

The longest-serving democratic leader in the Athenian democracy was Pericles, who made the Delian League an empire and later led that Athenian empire during the first two years of the Peloponnesian War. Pericles was a popular leader who led the citizens in the arts and literature and made Athens a center of learning.[2] Considered one of the great

---

[1] J. Thorley, *Athenian Democracy*. New York, NY: Routledge, 2005; P. J. Rhodes, *A History of the Classical Greek World, 478–323 BC*. New York, NY: Wiley and Sons, 2011.

[2] Plutarch, *Life of Pericles*, chap. XIV–XXIII.

orators in Greek history, Pericles's Funeral Oration celebrating fallen soldiers is one of the most remarkable speeches ever given. The following quotes are a testimony to the brilliance and eloquence of the democratic Pericles:

> *Freedom is the sure possession of those alone who have the courage to defend it.*
>
> *Just because you do not take an interest in politics doesn't mean politics won't take an interest in you.*
>
> *What you leave behind is not what is engraved in stone monuments, but what is woven into the lives of others.*

Trump is anti-Pericles. He has no ambitions to make the people of the United States more intelligent and more democratic. There is not an element of eloquence in Trump. True eloquence is good speech combined with passion and truth. Trump is no Pericles. His highest ambition seems to be to secure "love" for his brand as a person, but ultimately this is a losing battle because that which last is indeed woven in people's hearts.

The Age of Pericles is the opposite of the Age of Trump. Whereas only a third of the American people approved of Trump doing his first year as president, he claimed far more than he had achieved and apparently plotted to retain his office through a personal universe where he assumed the people were stupid.

As bizarre as it may seem to some, most Americans *know* stupid, and they know deplorable; democracies react to demagogues who seek compliance at all levels. No demagogue has ever secured a lasting positive reputation in history. The poisoned self-interest of demagogues is the seed of their destruction. Trump's political end and moral demise represent a flaw in his character, not a failure of the system.

The biographer Plutarch tells the world that Pericles stood first among the Athenians for forty years as the leader of Athens, from when he was about thirty-five years old. The middle of the fifth century BCE belonged to the leader of the democracy. Pericles was not flamboyant. He became a great model for judicious decisions, wisdom, frugality, and privacy, evidencing the ultimate judgment of history of those leaders who try their best to promote decency, justice, harmony, unity, balance, and order.[3]

Inexact and fractured as it was from the beginning, the Declaration of Independence, written principally by Thomas Jefferson, held within it the promises that could become the legitimate basis for protest and progress. On the other hand, the Constitution of the United States, fathered by James Madison, outlined the form of government for the people of the United States.

Thomas Jefferson and James Madison envisioned a system of government of the people, by the people, and for the people, where eligible people are elected to represent the people. In effect, they were flawed democrats and capitalists whose philosophy constantly conflicted with their actions.

We are able to feel a sense of personal growth in the intellectual and moral character of Jefferson, whose most famous quotes may be these:

> *The tree of liberty must be refreshed from time to time with the blood of patriots and tyrants.*
>
> *Honesty is the first chapter in the book of wisdom.*
>
> *In matters of style, swim with the current; in matters of principle, stand like a rock.*

If you examined Trump in the context of these statements, you would see the difference between a demagogue and a democrat. The tree of liberty must always be protected from demagogues by the vigorous defense provided by rational thinking. Furthermore, lying to the public, as Trump has done thousands of times, will eventually unsettle the masses to the point where he will be chastised by the democratic process. One thing that seems certain is that the democratic norms, though buffeted by malicious turbulence, are resilient.

Patriots must have some skin in the game, but during the rise of Trump, we have seen very few patriots on the side of the Republicans willing to

---

[3]Donald Kagan, *Pericles of Athens and the Birth of Democracy*. New York, NY: The Free Press, 1991.

fight the demagogue; they have been most willing to acquiesce. Yet a few Republican senators, especially Jeff Flake and John McCain, both from Arizona, have warned the nation about the political climate created by Trump's antics and ideas.

In October 2017, when McCain received the Liberty Medal for public service from the National Constitution Center in Philadelphia, Pennsylvania, he warned about the United States moving toward "half-baked, spurious nationalism." From his political platform as one who has been in national leadership, McCain warned that America should not fear the world that it has led for a nearly a hundred years and abandon "the ideals we have advanced around the globe." McCain said that the United States should not "refuse the obligations of international leadership . . . for the sake of some half-baked, spurious nationalism cooked up by people who would rather find scapegoats than solve problems."

Trump's State of the Union speech was generously sprinkled with elements of narcissism and authoritarianism. As a demagogue, he tries to place himself in the position of determining what others should do, and if he senses that people are opposing him, then he attacks like a wounded animal.

Trump called Democratic legislators treasonous simply because they would not applaud a line in his speech where he claimed to have done something that did not originate on his own watch, which shows the gall of the demagogue. Why should those who know that he did not create the conditions for the improvement in African American employment stand and applaud his usurpation of President Barack Obama's legacy? The willful lying and creative obfuscation of the truth show the dangerous capabilities of a person whose values completely reside in self-praise.

So Trump gave his first State of the Union address and could not resist the urge to wrap himself in the fabrics designed and created by another president. In many ways, this reminds me of the fascination that Turkish president Recep Tayip Erdogan has with Ataturk. When I visited Turkey, traveling from Istanbul to Ankara and back to Bodrum, everywhere I went, I felt that the legacy of the great Ataturk was under threat by the current president. The fact is that Ataturk, the great reformer of Turkey, has been dead since 1938! Trump's attack was on his immediate predecessors.

Trump's speech to the U.S. Congress was filled with the shameful rhetoric of a would-be demagogue who felt threatened by opponents who did not applaud his proposals.

Senator Flake condemned Trump for saying that the Democrats who didn't applaud his State of the Union address were "treasonous." Flake added, "Treason is not a punch line." As a demagogue would do, Trump took the lack of applause by Democrats for his speech as a personal insult; he said that they were "un-American[4]."

Senator Flake also claimed that the demagogue did not know the meaning of the word "treason" and, furthermore, did not appreciate the power of presidential words. "I have seen the president's most ardent defenders use the now-weary argument that the president's comments were meant as a joke, just sarcasm, only tongue in cheek," Flake said.[5] "As members of Congress, we must not ever accept undignified discourse as normal because of the requirements of tribal party politics."

The tone for a negative discourse, dishonesty, and narcissistic rhetoric is set by Trump's demagogic manner of speech. The habit of lying remains at the core of all Trump's rhetorical misdeeds. He is skillful at creating false information, disinformation, and half-truths in a way that has rarely been seen in presidential politics.

If honesty is the first chapter in the book of wisdom, then Trump is wandering around outside the library. He has not opened the introductory book of wisdom because his speech has become synonymous with that of a liar. Trump apparently sees lying as a functional part of governing because with the lie one is able to follow the pessimistic strategies of the late Roger Ailes and Roger Stone. They became infamous for creating political dramas that could be followed by political audiences. Ailes had been an advisor for Richard Nixon, George H. W. Bush, and other Republicans, including Rudy Giuliani. He is considered as one of the

---

[4]Daniella Diaz, "Flake Calls Out Trump for Saying Non-Clapping Democrats Are Treasonous," CNN *Politics*, February 6, 2018.

[5]ibid.

initiators of the Orchestra Pit Theory, which poses this question: "If you have two guys on a stage and one guy says, 'I have a solution to the Middle East problem' and the other guy falls in the orchestra pit, who do you think is going to be on the evening news?"[6]

WATCHING FOR DESPOTS

We are accustomed to calling Madison the other brain of the founding American documents. The *Declaration of Independence* was written in 1776 and the Americans subsequently created the *Articles of Confederation* in 1777 to hold the country together. This Confederation lasted for ten years, and then the Constitution of the United States of America was written in 1788 and ratified in 1789. The aging Benjamin Franklin was asked at the close of the Constitutional Convention as he left the Independence Hall on the final day of deliberations in 1787, "Well doctor, what have we got—a republic or a monarchy?" Franklin looked squarely into the person's eyes and said, "A republic, if you can keep it."

Trump is neither a Jefferson nor a Madison. Jefferson was an intellectual, gifted with the ability to marshal his talents to construct an eloquent response to the British Empire, despite his own collusion with the enslavement of Africans. Madison found the strength of character and the mental agility to write *The Federalist Papers*, alongside Alexander Hamilton, despite his inability to rein in Andrew Jackson's racist proclivities against the Native Peoples. Trump, on the other hand, has not displayed an intellectual theory of governing, a political ideology, or a philosophical curiosity about how to make a nation better. Rather, he has acted like a despot, even going to the extent of deliberately misleading the public with calls, for example, for the investigation of the FBI and the CIA. Trump stated that he wanted the DOJ to investigate if a spy had been embedded in his campaign. In fact, he "demanded" such an action

---

[6]Carl T. Bogus, *The Death of an Honorable Profession*, Indiana University Law School, March 17, 1997.

in the same way that some Eastern European autocrat would direct his underlings to act. Trump sees government as one man's complete rule, but democracy is by definition rule by the people.

Demagogues are not known to be thinkers; they are merely narcissistic actors. On the other hand, dictators have an interest in governing and in the theory of government; they could be beneficent or malevolent.

As Trump has no particular insight into political theory or history, he can easily become an unwitting puppet of either foreign operatives or the American oligarchs who represent his class interests. I am not even certain that he cares about the writing of laws since he seemed so distant from every piece of legislation that landed on his desk. He is simply a rubber stamp in search of numbers to feed his hunger for political love. Perhaps, the one action that he has taken consistently is to reverse every Obama executive order and to sign his own orders.

Power attracts many people who are easily beguiled by the quest; others are corrupted by holding office, and many of them are not worthy of the power that they gain. Misuse of the people's trust is almost predictable because the oligarchs, especially those who are wealthy, waste no time in drinking from the wells of public funds to make themselves richer.

I recall how elegantly, and eloquently former president Barack Obama pleaded with Americans to defend democracy in his farewell speech given in Chicago on January 10, 2017. He said,

> After eight years as your president, I still believe that. And it's not just my belief. It's the beating heart of our American idea—our bold experiment in self-government. It's the conviction that we are all created equal, endowed by our Creator with certain unalienable rights, among them life, liberty, and the pursuit of happiness. It's the insistence that these rights, while self-evident, have never been self-executing—that we, the people, through the instrument of our democracy, can form a more perfect union.

> This is the great gift our Founding Fathers gave us—the freedom to chase our individual dreams through our sweat, toil, and imagination and the imperative to strive together as well to achieve a greater good.

The demagogue is incapable of such words because the demagogue does not believe in these fundamental ideas. Instead of striving for the greater good, the demagogue strives for his own glory, encouraged by the "dilly-dilly" of his acolytes.

The country's first Black president was elected in 2008 on a message of hope and change; he was then reelected in 2012 as the people showed an authentic desire for a democratic state. He had ambition, confidence, and boldness in the face of issues, but he was neither petty nor unwise.

Trump vowed to undo many of Obama's signature policies, but as former vice president Joe Biden said on February 6, 2018, in an interview with CNN's Chris Cuomo, Trump would not be able to reverse all of the achievements of the Obama years but would try to do his best to damage the goods.

One of the more controversial proposals that Trump made during the first part of 2018 was for a military parade like the ones in France, China, Russia, and North Korea. Not only is this something that runs contrary to American tradition over the past fifty years, it is something that Trump embraces from the most authoritarian part of his brain. He is a demagogue who seeks military exhibitionism as a reflection of his strength. Showing off military might, regardless of how much money it will cost, is merely a display of his bravado.

PATRIARCHY AND ARROGANCE

Trump has a patriarchal temperament that is expressed in his arrogance in attempting to discredit the DOJ and the FBI. But it is also a part of his pomposity derived from his running beauty pageants and working as a television personality. Nothing escapes his patriarchal tenacity. Trump does not worry about anything but nationalism and populism, and hence he tries to divide the people, us against them, one against another, in order to maintain his control over a declining political base.

A demagogue is not a role model and must never be seen as someone whose behavior is admirable. This holds true especially because of Trump's declaration that people voted for him even when they had heard about his misdeeds and attitude toward women. A demagogue gathers all moral judgments from himself to himself; he is wrapped in a robe of incredulity. One hears him, sees him, and rushes to check with neighbors, friends, and family what one has heard precisely. What gives Trump, the demagogue, the authority to say that when people "deny" that they sexually harassed women they must be given a pass? It is nothing short of a patriarchal prerogative in Trump's mind. He has no moral compass that one would expect of a president of the United States.

Patriarchy has distorted the nature of right and wrong in the political era of Trump. In fact, Trump sides with those who act like him, talk like him, and think like him. A demagogue learns quickly that there is a certain segment in a democracy that will acquiesce to any type of leadership. There is nothing in history that tells us that a demagogue will not be acceptable to a certain minority of the electorate. They see in the demagogue the "father figure" who will take care of every problem and all issues that plague society. It is the glow of the patriarch that covers the inadequacies of the votarists.

All indications from those who have accused Trump of seeking to degrade women are that he is a regular abuser of women, which means that he does not believe the stories of women victims who accuse men of harassment or domestic violence. He defended Bill O'Reilly, Roger Ailes, Roy Moore, and other alleged abusers by saying that they "denied" the accusations. According to him, if you "deny," you will likely beat any charges, at least in the public eye. Of course, several women have accused Trump of sexual harassment. These violations remain one of the complications of the Trump presidency. Trump sees men who are patriarchs as allied with his views of society.

Patriarchy is a system of power of men over women that contains the elements of hegemony and domination. As a political system, patriarchy excludes women or keeps them in minor roles because men see themselves as the natural leaders in government, society, and the family. With such a male-oriented focus, the demagogue, who celebrates the domination of women, resonates with those who see the exploitation of those considered weaker as a natural occurrence. Such a position is the essence of gender chauvinism.

Great nations throw off despotic governments. We are always responsible for our political condition, and when we are confronted with despots, we must refuse domination. Trump aims to muddy the waters of national discourse by lying about anything that will make him look bad. He apparently does not care that his lies are the source of most of his political problems; however, the reaction to Trump has been strong from those who believe that he is a danger to democracy.

CHAPTER 4
The Fragility of Civility

Americans have come to accept the president as the commander-in-chief as well as the moral leader of the nation. Sadly, Donald Trump has shown himself to be out of his league as both a respected commander and a model of morality. When you cannot depend on the president's words or take cues about dignity, balance, order, race relations, and values from the actions of a president who speaks and behaves in public like a hooligan and a bully, it demeans the public and creates a society that is rough, rude, and disrespectful in relationships. My mail carrier said, "If the president is an idiot, then the people who elected him must be idiots." I would never go that far, but I do believe that if the president is a liar, then those who elected him, knowing that he lies, must also accept lying as a matter of principle. If the president is a misogynist and homophobe, then those who elected him must harbor those sentiments, we believe. The fragility of the American civil society is in the hands of diverse institutions, but the institution of the presidency is certainly one of the most important when it comes to sustaining principled government. The slow slide into corrupt, immoral, petty political machinations has been going on for a while, but Trumpism has accelerated the demise of decency.

Let us examine how Trump relates to others. Here is a partial list of the negative nicknames and epithets he has used:

Dicky Durbin for Senator Richard Durbin (D-Ilinois)

Al Frankenstein for Senator Al Franken (D-Minnesota)

Sneaky Diane Feinstein for Senator Diane Feinstein (D-California)

Sloppy Steve Bannon for Trump's own chief political strategist

Low Energy Jeb for former Florida governor Jeb Bush

Little Marco for Senator Marco Rubio (R-Florida)

Crying Chuck Schumer for Senator Chuck Schumer (D-New York)

Sleepy Eyes Chuck Todd for the NBC and MSNBC *Meet the Press* host.

Lyin' Ted for Senator Ted Cruz (R-Texas)

Crazy Bernie for Senator Bernie Sanders (I-Vermont)

Crooked Hillary for Democratic nominee, Hillary Clinton

Psycho Morning Joe for former Republican Congressman Joe Scarborough

Little Rocket Man for North Korean leader Kim Jong Un

Pocahontas for Senator Elizabeth Warren (D-Massachusetts)

Jeff Flakey for Senator Jeff Flake (R-Arizona)

Liddle Bob Corker for Senator Bob Corker (R-Tennessee)

Wacky Congresswoman Wilson for Congresswoman Fredericka Wilson

Little Adam Schiff for Congressman Adam Schiff (D-California)

There are scores of other names and epithets used by Trump to vilify his opponents and to entertain his followers, but when the hammer of public opinion or legal judgment falls on him, he will find few sympathizers among decent people. He provided his followers with an account filled with unsavory characteristics and embarrassing personal conflicts. Trump continued to cultivate a loyal patronage, erode institutional integrity, direct attacks on security organizations, debase civil servants, ridicule those who trust the political system, and undermine democracy by not confronting the Russian interference in American politics since his election. Indeed, his entire behavior as a campaigner and a president fits the pattern of a very petty person who could never consider any other person equal to or better than himself. Yet, as Bill Gates, one of the richest people in the world and one who is highly respected, pointed out, Trump did not know the difference between HIV and HPV. Trump's pettiness allows neither the ability to learn nor the ability to respect others.

This is one reason why Trump never gave a positive nickname to any other president. Bill Clinton, George W. Bush, and Barack Obama were all bad in his opinion. Only he was a superior person; only he knew how to be president. Everything that he could think of about his opponents seemed to be negative, and his language was filled with dignity-demeaning terminology. Running as fast as he could away from dignity-affirming categorization, Trump lands on the edges of negativity.

Legitimizing a demagogue is an insult to an informed democratic polity. Yet the demagogue used the cultural connection to the conservative movement to articulate his views. The vulnerable nature of democracy is revealed in how easily a foreign power using the pathways established by the people themselves can invade the electoral process. The demagogue, scared that admission of a foreign government's interference will call into question his election, claimed that it is a witch hunt for the DOJ (Department of Justice) to examine the Russian role in the American election, although more than 70 people and organizations had been charged as of 2018.

With an objective to knock out the pillars of democracy and the government institutions that place constraints on the executive, Trump started his administration stating that he did not believe all of the reports of Russian spying and involvement in the American election.[1] He demonstrated disrespect for all of the CIA operatives who had died on the job.[2]

Without any analytical documentation or critical appraisal, Trump claimed that he wanted to reconstruct the FBI and the DOJ. It is not clear if Trump was simply setting up actions that he could claim as something done by his narcissistic self or if he actually believed that these hallowed institutions needed change. Governance is always best when there is deliberation, and this means consultation with others who are experts. This does not mean that an executive cannot act; it simply means that the executive should act after taking advice.

---

[1]These are some of the statements that Trump made over time on the issue. He tweeted on February 18, 2018,

> I never said Russia did not meddle in the election, I said "it may be Russia, or China or another country or group, or it may be a 400 pound genius sitting in bed and playing with his computer." The Russian "hoax" was that the Trump campaign colluded with Russia—it never did!

Furthermore, while on Air Force One, speaking to reporters on November 2017, Trump said of Putin, "Every time he sees me, he says, 'I didn't do that, and I really believe that when he tells me that, he means it.'" In September 2016, in a debate with Democratic contender Hillary Clinton, Trump said,

> She's saying Russia, Russia, Russia, but I don't—maybe it was. I mean, it could be Russia, but it could also be China. It could also be lots of other people. It also could be somebody sitting on their bed that weighs 400 pounds, okay?

[2]Robin Wright, writing in the *New Yorker* on January 22, 2017, in an article titled "Trump's Vainglorious Affront to the CIA," says,

> In his remarks, Trump made passing reference to the 'special wall' behind him but never mentioned the top-secret work or personal sacrifices of intelligence officers like Ames and the others who died in Beirut, including the C.I.A. station chief Kenneth Haas, and James F. Lewis, who had been a prisoner of war in North Vietnam, and his wife Monique, who was on her first day on the job at the Beirut embassy. Nor did the President refer to any of the dozens of others for whom stars are etched on the hallowed C.I.A. wall of honor. It was like going to the Tomb of the Unknown Soldier and not mentioning those who died in the Second World War.

In some senses, the electoral process, a coin of modern democracy, is also one of its weakest links when it comes to the ambition of the demagogue. It is possible that democracies will be attacked in the future by a conspiratorial strategy of demagogic rhetoric and technological intrusions. The adaptation to assaults on democratic institutions will demonstrate the vulnerability that is built into the American system. Fierce battles to control the mechanisms of electoral politics will catapult the demagogue into a clearer view where the profile of ignorance, catastrophic divisiveness, and crudeness will render the society *awake* to social and political trouble.

History is no joke; it always has lessons to teach. Adolf Hitler and the National Socialists lost the presidential election of 1932 in Germany, but President Paul von Hindenburg later appointed Hitler as chancellor. He moved quickly to change the cabinet and to clamp down on opponents. Hindenburg later paved the way to dictatorship and war by issuing the Reichstag Fire Decree, which nullified civil liberties. After a series of parliamentary elections and associated backroom intrigues, Hitler emerged as the supreme leader, surrounded by a cadre of his political operatives who were willing to struggle to attain and maintain power in Germany. Ridding the various ministries and the cabinet of politicians and civil servants who had served previous governments, Hitler was able to root out many anti-Nazi officials. Trump's notion of a "deep state" may have come from some of his nationalistic strategists, who saw the progressive tendencies of a liberal-leaning state structure operating in the interest of civil rights, health rights, and protection of nature and against corporatist policies that crowd the rich with more wealth while failing to support the good of the public order by taxing the wealthy to build a better society. Getting to the bottom of this "deep state" has meant loading the judges' seats with some who are white nationalists, antipeople politicians, and racists who neither love nor respect the diverse society that the United States has become.

The demagogue enjoys using militaristic and physical metaphors and examples. When Trump as a candidate for the presidency spoke of beating up, knocking out, and pushing arrested people into police cars without protecting their heads and sent out calls to "lock her up" in reference to Hillary Clinton, he was exhibiting one of the features of the authoritarian personality. Trump strikes either when he feels under siege or when he wants to knock out his opponents before he is under siege. In other words, his entre character is wrapped up in the martial posture of attack. He supports himself by dragging out fake news stories and then condemning the mainstream news companies as the purveyors of fake news. This is a sinister political and rhetorical assault on what is considered the foundation of a democratic society. For Trump, all news should show him as he sees himself, that is, as a great person, or else it should be attacked.

Civility is a thin thread in human society; it is not a rope that can hold when it has to bear the weight of thousands of lies. Civility breaks in the face of the constant propaganda of lies. It causes people to want to fight, to defend their dignity, and to recoil at the slightest provocation. The use of fake news by a demagogue confirms that he has no sympathy or empathy for those who are mangled in the iron jaws of lies. A demagogue will sacrifice the institutions of liberty for the sake of his self-aggrandizement. All conversation and actions are important to the demagogue only so far as they underscore his special genius.

Trump mastered the propaganda technique of getting ahead of his opponent by announcing that any news that showed him in a negative light was "fake news." Of course, he also criticized information that demonstrated that his policy ideas were not grounded in reality. The problem with demagogues is that all news that aims to set the record straight after they have lied is called fake news. But what is fake news?

Fake news is a kind of propaganda that uses misinformation, lies, fabrications, and hoaxes to blind people to the truth. A fake news operator is likely to throw so much misinformation into the atmosphere that the person receiving the news will be completely befuddled. A brand of fake news is broadcast, printed, or distributed over social media as a deliberate instrument of political confusion. Gaining politically or financially from falsehoods spread abroad is the main purpose of fake news. Those who intentionally mislead others with information that is inauthentic and used only to serve the political interests of the demagogue are the worst attackers of democratic institutions because they corrupt the very ground on which the trees of security and respect grow in society.

A particularly dangerous aspect of the "fake news" controversy since the days of Trump has been the fact that the demagogue has mastered the technique of creating his own reality and then passing it off as if it is real and all other information, although gathered by reputable media agencies, is fake. One can only do this with a certain type of boldness in order to convince the masses that they actually do not see what they see. It is like his defense of the sexual abusers who hide behind denial.

The demagogue succeeds at this because all demagogues have mastered human behavior. During his rise to celebrity, Trump, it is claimed, often called in to radio stations or other media to give the host positive reports about himself. He knew the habits of media institutions and the need for something new and exciting all the time. Thus, he would disguise his voice and call a station supporting the idea that Donald Trump was smart, great, and intelligent when it came to business. People who did not know that Trump was a manipulator of the media found him to be credible and a person of goodwill.

Demagogues also know that ratings bring in advertisers and advertisers make money for the media companies. We now know that Facebook News Feeds and other media instruments have played into the hands of the fake news creators. There are several dangers in this scenario, each one capable of taking down a government or a president. The first is the ease with which young people can get access to false information often contradicting what they learn legitimately in school. The second is the cooptation of the news feeds by hostile actors on the world stage who create false information and market it by circulating it on legitimate news services as if it were real. Almost no American demagogue before Trump has had such easy access to millions of people. His calculus has to be that his millions of followers on Twitter who are exposed to his lies and created stories will never abandon him.

I have found that fake news now competes with real news for the attention of large groups of people. During the 2016 presidential campaign, fake news groups probably from a hostile nation sent out false political information to African Americans in an attempt to disrupt the strong Hillary Clinton advocacy group. It was reported in May 2018 that Steve Bannon, erstwhile Trump advisor and white nationalist, had worked to suppress the Black vote in the 2016 election. Although we know that many people acted on this information, whether to hold rallies or spread the anti-Clinton propaganda through social media, we are yet unsure about whom to precisely implicate. Russia has been accused, but it has been suggested in some circles that the Russian trolls may have operated with the support, explicit or implicit, of the Trump campaign. I believe that Buzzfeed found that many fake news stories about the presidential campaign of 2016 had received more social media interaction than the top 20 legitimate news stories by reputable companies. One explanation of this credibility and information phenomenon may be that the fake news items are not fact-checked, edited, or discussed on editorial boards. In other words, there are no rules to which the fake news hawker has to adhere. In these cases, the American masses are like ducks in a pond being fed anything that is thrown in by passers-by. How do you tell bread from crud if it has the same color and consistency?

Fake news can spread by word of mouth. African Americans are no strangers to the use of lies to stir up whites against Blacks. At the dawn of the twentieth century and culminating around 1919, more than four thousand African people were lynched at the hands of white mobs. In many cases, these mobs had been agitated by the spread of fake news that Black men had raped white women. One of the worst events was the bombing of "Black Wall Street," a prosperous area of Tulsa, Oklahoma, after a report that a Black elevator operator had raped a white girl. It was later proved to be false, but by the time the truth was reported, many Blacks and whites had been killed and Black businesses had been bombed from the air.

Fake news is not new, but if a demagogue cannot control the legitimate media, he will condemn it while claiming that he has the only true news. The demagogue seeks to isolate the masses from other influences and is frustrated when his words are contested by other sources. The challenge is problematic for the demagogue because he never wants to engage in logical debate over policy; he would rather dictate policy.

THE DANGER OF DEMAGOGUERY AND LIES

During the European Medieval Period in 1475, it is said that a false report went out in Trent, Italy, that some Jews had murdered a young

Christian child named Simonino.[3] The report created such hysteria that many Jews were arrested and fifteen were burned alive. Pope Sixtus tried to quell the story, but it had already infiltrated the outer reaches of the city. This so-called "blood libel" story was frequently the cause of pogroms in Europe. People were eager to hear that Jews drank the blood of Christian children, using this as an excuse to persecute and murder innocents. Consequently, students of human behavior have often spoken of the fickleness of stability in societies. As a student of communication and later as head of the communication department at SUNY, Buffalo, I came to learn that powerful, incisive, and emotional rhetoric in the hands of a demagogue or despot could cause cities to be razed, lead to the murder of religious leaders and innocent people, and drive mobs to commit the most awful crimes.

Journalistic ethics evolved in Europe during the period after the invention of the printing press in 1436. Although the demand for references and citations increased after the trial of Galileo Galilei in 1610, the printing press had already given historians a new instrument for cross-checking. News and information were considered so important that purveyors of fake news were often banned and sometimes fined for their lies. One of the most famous cases was that of the Dutchman Gerard Lodewijk van der Macht, who was banned four times by the Dutch until he eventually left for America. Some historians have claimed that Benjamin Franklin wrote false stories about "murderous scalping

---

[3]In "The Long and Brutal History of Fake News," *Politico*, December 18, 2016, it was succinctly put that

> the fake news hit Trent, Italy, on Easter Sunday, 1475. A 2½-year-old child named Simonino had gone missing, and a Franciscan preacher, Bernardino da Feltre, gave a series of sermons claiming that the Jewish community had murdered the child, drained his blood and drunk it to celebrate Passover. The rumors spread fast. Before long da Feltre was claiming that the boy's body had been found in the basement of a Jewish house. In response, the Prince-Bishop of Trent Johannes IV Hinderbach immediately ordered the city's entire Jewish community arrested and tortured.

Indians" in service to King George III to sway the public toward supporting the American Revolution. In my doctoral dissertation, "Samuel Adams and the Rhetoric of Revolution," at the University of California, Los Angeles, I examined the essays written by Adams in the *Boston Gazette* and discovered that the essays were often over the top in terms of the reasons advanced for a revolution. Indeed, there was hardly any real reason for the colonists to resist Great Britain since they were not taxed as hard as the people who remained in Britain and had much more liberty than them.

Fake news has been the cause of some of the worst tragedies in human history. It seems that it a part of the politics in a democracy, and hence we must always call into question the safeguards that we have put in place to prevent absolute chaos. Consider that Marie Antoinette was beheaded because her face had been printed on a canard in 1793.

In an effort to teach the masses how to recognize fake news, the International Federation of Library Associations and Institutions pub-lished a list of criteria that should be used to assess information. Specifically, the Federation says that the public should

1. consider the source (to understand its mission and purpose),
2. read beyond the headline (to understand the whole story),
3. check the authors (to see if they are real and credible),
4. assess the supporting sources (to ensure that they support the claims),
5. check the date of publication (to see if the story is relevant and up-to-date),
6. ask if it is a joke (to determine if it is meant to be satire),
7. review your own biases (to see if they are affecting your judgment), and
8. ask experts (to get confirmation from independent people with knowledge).

I am a believer in media literacy and think that it will be a good idea for departments of communication and general education in the United States to teach fact-checking skills to students and ordinary citizens as a way to train the masses in vetting processes for journalistic output.

CHAPTER 5

The Promises to the People

Demagogues have been so plentiful throughout the world that they have established very obvious patterns, tactics, and forms of communication. There are many methods by which demagogues have manipulated and incited crowds throughout history. No one demagogue uses them all, and no two demagogues use exactly the same methods to gain popularity and loyalty from the people. Even ordinary politicians use some of these techniques from time to time; a politician who failed to stir emotions at all would have little hopes of being elected. What these techniques have in common, and what distinguishes demagogues' use of them, is the consistent use of tactics to shut down reasoned deliberation by stirring up overwhelming passions in people. Trump's campaign rallies were often cries for blood, the throwing, so to speak, of red meat, to followers, who barked for more. He basked in his followers' love of his often vile rhetoric of hate.

Sometimes, a genuinely wise politician, one who seeks not his or her own aggrandizement but works for the good of the people, may speak in ways that represent demagogic rhetoric to "fight fire with fire." A statesperson usually is calm, cool, and calculating, but a demagogue is always exciting and emotional even when the tone is quiet. There is danger in a politician taking up the methods of the demagogue; one can lose a sense of perspective and moral compass. Once a politician has decided to "out demagogue" another politician, he or she is in moral trouble. Alabama governor George Wallace said that he once lost an election because his opponent "outsegged" him, meaning that the opponent went to the well of racism and segregation much more than Wallace did. His response was that he would never allow another candidate to "out-segg" him. In fact, both Spiro Agnew of Maryland, who went on to become vice president under Richard Nixon, and Winthrop Roosevelt of Arkansas, claimed that their opponents had "out-segged" them. This meant that the white politician who appealed to the segregationist element among white voters in the South had a better chance of winning in much of the twentieth century. Trump harks back to that day by trying to ensure that no other candidate goes to the bottom of the barrel quicker and more often than he does. This is his sad expectation in a deeply racist nation.

He who throws down the gauntlet first establishes the position for the opposition. But the person who takes up the gauntlet understands that defiance is necessary to defend personal and sometimes collective integrity. This is why people cannot allow any demagogue to assume that they are weak, insignificant, or waiting for a savior. In a democracy, the people must pick up the gauntlet thrown down by a demagogue and run toward confrontation with their shields of truth, dignity, and self-sacrifice.

PROPAGANDA AND DEMAGOGUERY

After World War I, when propaganda became a major part of warfare, Edward Filene in 1937 created the Institute of Propaganda Analysis with the idea of educating the American public about propaganda techniques. Filene and his colleagues identified seven strategies used by propagandists:

1. *Name calling:* The propagandist uses negative or discriminatory terms to arouse prejudice or suspicion.
2. *Glittering generalities:* The propagandist employs slogans or simple catchphrases with themes of honor, love, dignity, peace, family values, freedom, and patriotism.

3. *Transfer:* This technique makes use of a beloved symbol, like the national flag, to win popular approval.
4. *Testimonial:* This means that the propagandist employs testimonials from authority figures or celebrities to make an association with a cause.
5. *Plain folks:* The idea here is to convince people that the person is like them and shares their issues and concerns.
6. *Bandwagon:* The propagandist uses this technique to play on the human desire to be a part of a group, a crowd, or an important team.
7. *Card stacking:* In using the card-stacking technique, the propagandist can cherry pick the arguments to make it seem that the propagandist way is the only correct one.

These techniques are associated with propaganda, but as you can see, a skilled demagogue such as Trump employs these tactics in offensive moves against those he considers opponents. Trump has used every one of these propaganda techniques during his presidency. But, perhaps more to the point, he has employed the techniques most associated with demagogic speech. These techniques have been developed over the past fifty years or more and have been based on studying the models of Adolf Hitler's Propaganda Ministry and Senator Joseph McCarthy's House Un-American Activities Committee.

Thus, the main techniques are scapegoating, fearmongering, lying, emotional oratory and personal charisma, accusation of weakness, promising the impossible, violence and physical intimidation, personal insults, vulgarity, ordinary folk actions, and simplification of ideas.

Scapegoating

The most fundamental demagogic technique is probably scapegoating blaming a group's economic and social problems on an out-group, usually of a different race, religion, or social class. For example, McCarthy (R-Wisconsin) claimed that all of the problems of the U.S. resulted from "communist subversion." Denis Kearney, known for his violently anti-Chinese rhetoric and racial agitation, blamed all the problems of white

laborers in California on Chinese immigrants.[1] Hitler blamed the Jews
and Roma for Germany's defeat in the first international European war
as well as for the economic troubles that came afterward. This was
central to his appeal. Many people said that the only reason they liked
Hitler was because he was against the Jews. Fixing blame on the Jews
gave Hitler a way to intensify his sense of personal messianism; he
would save the Germans from the Jews.

The rhetorical claims made about the scapegoated class are transgenera-
tional, transcontinental, and transcultural. This appears to be the case
even if the demagogue and the scapegoated group have little interaction
with each other. It seems that the idea is to have a group to blame.
Demagogues can have serial scapegoats; when one group is no longer
effective in raising the opposition, the demagogue looks for another
group to attack.

------

[1]In 1878, Kearney gave a speech that included these words:

> To add to our misery and despair, a bloated aristocracy has sent to
> China—the greatest and oldest despotism in the world—for a cheap work-
> ing slave. It rakes the slums of Asia to find the meanest slave on earth—
> the Chinese coolie—and imports him here to meet the free American in
> the Labor market, and still further widen the breach between the rich
> and the poor, still further to degrade white Labor.
>
> These cheap slaves fill every place. Their dress is scant and cheap. Their
> food is rice from China. They hedge twenty in a room, ten by ten. They
> are wipped curs, abject in docility, mean, contemptible and obedient in all
> things. They have no wives, children or dependents.
>
> They are imported by companies, controlled as serfs, worked like slaves, and
> at last go back to China with all their earnings. They are in every place, they
> seem to have no sex. Boys work, girls work; it is all alike to them.

The father of a family is met by them at every turn. Would he get work for himself? Ah! A stout Chinaman does it cheaper. Will he get a place for his oldest boy?
He cannot. His girl? Why, the Chinaman is in her place too! Every door is closed.
He can only go to crime or suicide, his wife and daughter to prostitution, and his
boys to hoodlumism and the penitentiary.

In American society, the group most susceptible to demagogues appear to be white Protestant Americans. They tend to see themselves as the "we" people, while Blacks, Jews, and Mexicans are viewed as "the others." It is impossible for the scapegoated to be moved to "we" because the others are responsible always for the troubles of "we."

The demagogue is keen to explain to his followers that the government has a "deep state" that must be cleaned out for him to be able to exercise his authority to support them. He leads on his followers with the idea that the Democrats are plotting against him and that all investigations into his personal finances, obstruction of legal processes, and collusion with Russians to undermine the campaign of Hillary Clinton are conspiracies against him.

Demagogues sometimes prefer to use the pronoun "they" to speak of the unnamed opposition. All those referred to as "they" are sexual predators, rapists, gangsters, members of M-13, and dangerous killers. This is the rhetoric that stirs up the demagogue's followers, who believe that their women would be raped and their lives would be in danger if the nation allowed immigrants into the country. Doom is sure to envelop the nation if the people do not give the demagogue more power and more adulation. The solution for this is to deny the demagogue the oxygen of admiration for unethical, trifling, and irrational behavior.

Fearmongering

Many demagogues have risen to power by spreading information and misinformation intended to frighten audiences. Trump went directly for one of the most obvious and sick attacks by warning people that "Mexicans are rapists."

African Americans have seen this story before. Jews know this tactic. Any people who have been labeled the "other" know that the demagogue's cry that "they will rape your daughters" is one of the most used tactics against African American males.

The American demagogue Pitchfork Ben Tillman at the turn of the twentieth century often evoked colorful and pathetic racist imagery describing in vivid detail Black men lurking about to rape white women. In Tillman's rhetoric, the Black man had an innate weakness of character that meant he had to be kept away from the white woman. Tillman, who was elected governor of South Carolina in 1890 and elected senator repeatedly from 1895 to 1918, was one of the most virulent purveyors of demagogic hatred against African Americans.

Trump may have never known Tillman, but his techniques, especially against Mexicans, is not far from Tillman's thinking about Africans.

Lying

The demagogue uses lies as an effective instrument of people control. It is not just errors in policy or judgment but the absolute use of mendacity to influence the minds of his followers. Creating a web of lies to appeal to the emotions of his audiences seems to be a part of Trump's modus operandi. Lies create additional chaos in a demagogue's administration. Sometimes the lies of the demagogue are unexpected and often trap the liar in more chaos. He usually demonstrates little regard for the truth so long as he feels that his lies or those of his closest supporters benefit him politically. At some point, the bizarre maze of lies captures the demagogue in an endless game of explanations.

My assessment is that Trump is opportunistic. He will do whatever it takes to arouse emotions and win favor with audiences. If the people are believed to have a problem with any person or ideas, Trump will identify with their sentiments in an incessant chain of lies. It seems that Trump is a compulsive liar, seeking only to win friends, votes, and allegiances to him personally irrespective of the facts. If you are a demagogue who carefully monitors Twitter or Fox News for the most populist ideas, you are likely to create your own reality to the extent that the lies will support your personal glory.

In Trump's case, he was much like other American demagogues who used the big lie, the lie to the side, the lie on other people, and the informational lie. The big lie, Hitler's favorite, is used to express something that is so wildly incredible that people will say it must be true because who would be so foolish as to say that if it were not so. The lie to the side is one that supports the big lie, such as when Trump in explaining that "Mexico will pay for the wall" claimed that "in one way or another they will pay." He slips easily from the frontal lie to a smaller version of the big lie. A lie on other people is when a liar claims that someone did something or said something or did not say something or do something. For example, Trump argued that former FBI director James Comey was not told to go easy on General Michael Flynn. Informational lies are used to confuse the audience with false data. When the demagogue wants to maintain a certain position that is contrary to what is known, he then tells a lie to establish a different number, set of facts, or reality.

One of the most classic cases of lying with impunity was when Senator Joe McCarthy of Wisconsin during the 1950s claimed to have "here in my hand" a list of 205 members of the Communist Party working in the U.S. Department of State. Not long after this claim, McCarthy decided that there were 57 "card-carrying Communists."[2]

McCarthy's challenge to the legislative branch of government was one of the most serious to confront the Senate. His colleagues pressed him to "give us the names," and then McCarthy told them that the records were unavailable to him, but he knew for a fact that there were "absolutely" 300 communists who were certified to the secretary of state for discharge but only 80 were actually fired. McCarthy changed his statement again and said that he had a real list of 81 communists that he would reveal later. This was all bluff, lies, and in the end, he never found a single communist in the Department of State.

THE TRUMP PLAYBOOK

Trump was never a politician before he ran for the presidency. He was in construction of major buildings throughout the world but mostly in Manhattan, New York. His claim to fame was based on the broad celebrity he acquired in running beauty pageants, acting in *The Apprentice*, and coauthoring the book *The Art of the Deal*, in which he offered his suggestions on how to negotiate a deal. Seeing him in the office of the president, one understands that a lot of what he called negotiation was about lying. No president has ever been accused of as many lies as Trump.

---

[2]McCarthy made a distinction between "card-carrying communists" and those who were just "fellow travelers."

The Washington Post says that Trump lied 2,000 times during his first year as president. One of the biggest lies was that "Mexico will pay for the wall" that he wanted to build on the border. Mexico immediately denied this lie, but he continued to use it to rally those who were ready for a hero. Lack of global knowledge, ignorance of politics, and willingness to believe someone who appears successful will get you a demagogue to play on your emotions while undermining the values of the nation.

Databases, centers, and institutes that categorize and track suspect political statements made by Trump estimated that through his Twitter account and public utterances Trump made an average of at least five false claims a day. Trump appears to make a variety of exaggerated and false claims when it comes to his position vis-à-vis other presidents. He loves to claim that he has done something that "no other president" has done, and most of the time the claims are false. However, the demagogue knows that audiences do not have ways to immediately fact check the information presented as correct. Some even proclaim, "The president does not need to lie because he has all of the information." Such trust in a demagogue is dangerous. The demagogue wins the trust of followers with lies like the following:

- "We can build the wall in one year, and we can build it for much less money than what they're talking about."
- On immigration policy, in the diversity visa lottery: "What's in their hands are the worst of the worst, but they put people in that they don't want into a lottery, and the United States takes those people."
- "We have tremendous numbers of people and drugs pouring into our country. So, in order to secure the border, we need a wall."

Trump's lies poured forth as if they were factual and authoritative, condemning his listeners to receive inaccurate and confusing information. Like most demagogues, Trump realizes that the less educated masses can be manipulated because they have no systematic understanding of reality. They are on opinion leaders for their facts and are apt to believe that rich people are smarter than other people, that white people are being deprived of their rights by Africans and Mexicans, and that the coal industry and shoe-making factories will return to the United States. With little or no understanding of economics, the changing nature of world powers, and the global conditions of trade, Trump's followers believe that the United States can and should dictate the terms of global markets and regional power blocs. That time has long passed, but the demagogue is able to appeal to his followers with the lie that he will make it happen again because he knows that the most ardent conservatives actually believe that his vision is possible, even if he does not believe in it himself.

This situation reminds me of John Moody, the Fox News executive editor and executive vice president, who wrote an op-ed on February 10, 2018, complaining that the American Winter Olympics team of 244 people needed to be less "darker, gayer, or different."[3] I guess the term "darker" referred to the 10 Blacks on the team and the term "gayer" referred to the two openly gay athletes, but I will not even proffer a guess on what he meant by "different."

Stupidity has no ethnicity, but it often seems quite popular among the ruling class white conservatives who sell a menu of conspiracies. Can you really imagine what emanates from a group whose leadership practices bad racial thinking? The devaluation of rational thought suggests that instead of trying to close the Corporation for Public Broadcasting, the National Endowment for the Humanities, and the National Endowment for the Arts, the Trump administration should have sought to raise the level of understanding in the nation. Democracy is lost when the citizenry loses faith in the words and pronouncements of the leaders of society. The number one leader in the United States in 2018 was President Trump, but to say that he is a liar gives others with such proclivities the right to express their own willingness to lie. Mendacious behavior is like snow; so lies can cover everything, but like snow they will melt if the sun is hot enough. When a racist New York City attorney named Aaron Schlossberg was accused of discrimination and yelling at immigrants who did not look like him or speak English as their first language, he was just channeling the Trump phenomenon against people who were not European.

---

[3]John Moody, "In Olympics, Let's Focus on the Winner of the Race—not the Race of the Winner" *Fox News Opinion*, February 10, 2018.

The Washington Post article of January 10, 2019, said that "Trump's claim about drug smuggling and the wall has been repeated 17 times, and by June, he had repeated it even more."[4] With no proof, Trump argued that building the wall would keep drugs from pouring into the country. In just two months into his administration, Trump falsely described the immigration diversity lottery more than 10 times. At the very beginning of his presidential campaign, Trump demagogued the wall and low-balled the cost of building such a monumental monstrosity between Mexico and the United States.

PRESIDENTIAL ENVY

However, given Trump's envy of former president Barack Obama, his most repeated claim was that the Affordable Care Act was dying or was essentially dead, when in fact the Congressional Budget Office was saying that the Obamacare exchanges were not imploding and remained stable with healthy enrollment. But Trump's assault on the Obamacare program was relentless until the legislators failed to repeal it. Regardless of how hobbled it had become because of the attempt on Trump's part to kill the mandate that every person should have health insurance, people still signed up for it at a faster rate than in the year before Trump's administration took office.

Given Trump's antipathy toward Obama, one wonders why he sought to repeatedly take credit for political, business, and social events that were started under the Obama administration. Many business decisions were made prior to his election, and yet he took advantage of the business actions of giant corporations. Several economic achievements were set in place by the Obama administration's rescue of the nation's key technological industries, especially the automobile industry, and the shoring up of the financial institutions that were teetering on absolute failure. One

---

[4]Glenn Kessler, Salvadore Rizzo, and Meg Kelly, "President Trump Has Made 10,796 False or Misleading Claims Over 869 Days," *Washington Post*, June 10, 2019. https://www.washingtonpost.com/politics/2019/06/10/president-trump-has-made-false-or-misleading-claims-over-days/.

can question, and people have, the idea that there were financial companies that were "too big" to fail. Nevertheless, the saving of the economy
from the depression of 2008–2009 must be attributed to the quick and
decisive actions of the Obama government.

One does not have to revisit Obama-era policies to see the inconsisten-
cies in the demagogue's rhetoric of simple lies. When Trump's tax law
was passed in 2017, it was demagogued when Trump claimed falsely
that it was the largest tax cut in history and that the United States had
the highest tax rates in the world. On January 30, 2018, *CNN Politics*
reported that Trump had overstated the facts with his boast. The CNN
researchers said, "But arguably, President Barack Obama passed a
larger tax cut by making most of President George W. Bush's cuts permanent. President Ronald Reagan definitely did. And Presidents John F.
Kennedy and Lyndon Johnson probably did, too." Furthermore, *CNN
Politics* said that "tax analysts have been unequivocal that Trump's
claim is not true."

I have concluded that Trump is adding a flavor to American demagoguery that we have not seen much in this relatively new century. The
obvious strategy is to tell many lies in a short period of time, like one
firing from a shotgun many pellets flying in a wide swath with a big
bang. Ordinary people do not know what to make of this: Are all of these
lies? They surmise, "It cannot be that everything the president says is a
lie, can it?" As a master of demagoguery, Trump also knows that the
media, despite its attempts, will not be able to fact-check everything he
says in real time. A lie lives with two legs for a while before one or both
legs are destroyed by truth. This is a game that should never be played in
a democracy but is always played by selfish politicians for personal
political gain.

EMOTIONAL ORATORY

Many demagogues have demonstrated remarkable skill at moving audiences to great emotional depths and heights during a single speech.
Sometimes this is due to exceptional verbal eloquence, sometimes to
personal charisma, and sometimes to both. Hitler demonstrated both in
his speeches to German audiences. Accordingly, stories abound that

Hitler's eyes hypnotized people, that they became immobilized because of his personal passion, and that he overwhelmed his audiences with his ability to voice what they wanted to say but feared to say. What demagogues do best is to allow people to believe that they are the voice that will represent them. From the most bitter racism and unspoken hatred to the colorful language that gives expression to them, the reactionary masses are able to pile onto the shoulders of the demagogue their dislikes, preferences, and foul language. They become like infants with their parents.

Communication scholars such as Fred Casmir and Erika Vora, as well as others, have categorized the rhetorical style of Hitler. He would begin his talks slowly, talking about his life as a child—drawing the people in with a slow style of speech that was almost boring until he raised the resonance—and then he would go into his blame game. Well, Trump did not come from a situation of poverty, and he does not have that story to tell, yet in many of his speeches, he minimizes the nature of his upbringing and emphasizes the idea that he had to work very hard. Rarely does he mention the fact that when you start off in a family with millions left to you, there is an advantage that the masses of Americans do not have. He did not suffer the humiliation that often comes with the lack of food or resources. Trump lived the life of a rich child who probably bullied other children who had less considering his current behavior. There is certainly nothing wrong with having been lucky enough to have successful parents, but there is something terribly wrong with trying to identify that fact as similar to the life of the coal miners of West Virginia or the potato farmers of Idaho. The problem with Trump is not his money or his silver spoon upbringing but his utter lack of empathy with the millions who yearn for enough resources to feed their families, to pay for health care, or to cross a border into a country that would give them a chance to succeed. Rather than support the human desires, wishes, and needs of the masses, Trump seeks ways to exploit the people.

Hitler shrieked hatred of Bolsheviks, Jews, Roma, Czechs, Poles, or whoever he claimed stood in his way—like Trump's modern rhetoric of mocking the disabled, criticizing those he thought were too fat, ridiculing those he considered too weak or too slow, and so forth, Hitler mastered the technique of ridiculing and insulting other people, sometimes telling his audiences that he would destroy such people. How could people we think of as reasonable and normal, maybe even religious, and pious, accept such a vile and poisonous rapport with a demagogue?

I suggest that Trump, like Hitler, was a student of human nature, and in Trump's case, his time in military school, his practice as a young bully, his brash and pompous behavior as a young man, and his adult life as a sexual predator according to his own words confirmed in his heart his ability to manipulate people through bluff.

Trump is not a natural orator; his appeal is based in his populist promises to an energetic minority that he would save them from the *others*. One does not have to master metaphors, similes, or any other elements of style to move those who seek relief from what they consider to be existential threats. Apparently, what one has to do is to give people the most wildly irrational promises and then pound that into their heads, even as a conspiracy theory, to the extent that they come to believe it more than the speaker, and you will have a following. We have seen this narrative with religious fanatics who claim the most irrational ideas with passion and then find other people willing to believe even to entering the Brand Davidian and James Warren Jones's Jonestown cults until their deaths.

ENTER RACE AS A TACTIC

What history teaches us is that race is often a fundamental part of the American demagogue's bag of tricks. In using the opposition of races rather than the uniting of races, Trump harks back to a nativist white American emotion. America's history is replete with anti-African demagogues such as James Kimble Vardaman, governor of Mississippi from 1904 to 1908 and senator from Mississippi from 1913 to 1919. When President Theodore Roosevelt invited African Americans to a White House reception, Vardaman railed, "Let Teddy take coons to the White House. I should not care if the walls of the ancient edifice should become so saturated with the effluvia from the rancid carcasses that a Chinch bug would have to crawl upon the dome to avoid asphyxiation." Like the speeches of most demagogues, Vardaman's speeches were often devoid of serious content as he preferred ceremonial talk even when the occasion called for deliberation and argument. His speeches were avenues for him to drive home his irrepressible hatred of African people.

The demagogues' appeal to deeply felt emotions has been known to win elections for them. They could even have opposition from the free press, seeking to tell the truth, and yet they are able to attract audiences who believe the lies, distractions, assaults, and broken promises peddled by the demagogues, who in most cases seek to create an autocracy.

Even as President Trump drowned out the media with his messages to his followers on Twitter, they experienced his tweets as words from the autocrat who denies them, within the context of his own universe, any other information. They wake up in the morning and go to bed at night intoxicated by the demagogue's prevarications. In a sly and deceitful twist to assaulting the media experts, Trump claimed that the main-stream media, all of the major traditional news agencies, did nothing but push "fake news" and the only true news was advanced by those who praised Trump.

It appears that the demagogue does not care about any fact even if the fact is known by millions of people; he is able to twist the information to support his reasoning. The only politics of the demagogue is the sav-ing of himself. This is why it is easy for him to say one thing in the morning and another at night. He is willing to use information, reveal any sources, conceal any incident, or weaponize classified information to protect his vanity.

Congress did not limit his abuses of power during the first year of Trump's administration. The legislators were weak and ineffective in stopping Trump from a steady diet of self-aggrandizement. Republicans, in leadership of the House and the Senate, seemed paralyzed or fright-ened to take on Trump.

What the American people witnessed with the election in 2016 of Trump was the capture of state power by a radical clique willing to destroy public institutions in education, justice, energy, health, and other sectors in order to create an autocracy where the "leader" can be glorified by marching bands and demonstrations of military armament. Steve Bannon, Breitbart's entrepreneurial white nationalist strategist, who would later leave the administration and go to France to peddle his racist ideas to the Le Pen crowd, was to be the grand master of Trump's rise to glory as the leader. Alas, it was not to be because demagogues must always appear to have a mind of their own, and some people thought and wrote that Bannon was Trump's mind.

In fifth century, BCE Greece, Cleon, like many demagogues who came after him, believed that to keep the people's loyalty he had to demonstrate brutality as a measure of his power. For the demagogue, talking, negotiating, and mediating show weakness that compromises the demagogue's persona of powerfulness. Cleon believed that people despise those who treat them well and fear those who show brutality. While demagogues like to make strength, especially brute force, one of their weapons to fight against enemies, logic does not hold in human communication. Most people love those who love them and despise those who despise them.

General Cleon opposed the idea of debating the issue of recalling the ships that he had sent the day before toward Mytilene to slaughter the population. He saw the debate as a sign of weak government. In fact, debating issues was considered the preoccupation of the idle and weak; for Cleon, the only reaction to enemies was to lock them up or kill them, and in this way, he argued, the people would see his strength. Through the centuries, there have been variations of this thinking despite the obvious truth that people prefer governments and governors who tell the truth, respect their person and their rights, and seek the higher ideals of life.

One variation to destroying enemies physically is destroying their reputations. Although Senator Joe McCarthy did not have evidence, he persistently claimed or insinuated that those who opposed him were communist sympathizers. McCarthy's line went like this: "I am for the American people, and the American people are against communism. I am against communism, and you are against me, so you must be a communist."

Trump used the demagogic technique of promising something so wild that he had no intention of really seeing it through but rather used it as a technique to arouse emotions. Should it become law in some form or another, he would claim it, but the emotional effect is all he was looking for in making the promise. This is why he had no idea of what it would cost or look like or which of his building contractor friends would revel in receiving a contract to build the wall between the United States and Mexico. Most demagogues give empty promises that they do not intend to fulfill.

Governor Huey Long of Louisiana was also one of the prominent demagogues of the twentieth century. He once promised during a campaign that if the people elected him president, he would give everyone a house, a car, a radio, and $2000 annually. He had no plan of doing this, yet thousands of people joined up with him in a Share-the-Wealth campaign as he sought to become president. Although never thought of as a rabid racist such as his son, Russell Long, would turn out to be, Huey Long nevertheless was a southerner with proclivities and attitudes on race based on the prohibitions placed on Blacks in Louisiana by the 1898 Constitution.

Trump obviously believed that he could promise anything because he knew that people would buy anything if you said it long enough and loud enough. They would even buy and do things against their own political and economic interests. Using his prior business success, Trump became, in his mind, the one who would solve all problems better than any previous president. I think that there is a certain callousness and cruelty in the exploitation of working-class people, miners, farmers, and ordinary citizens when they are given impossible promises.

During his campaign for the nomination and then the presidency, Trump encouraged his supporters to violently intimidate his opponents. This is a demagogic technique used to encourage loyalty and discourage anyone from opposing him. "Pitchfork" Ben Tillman used this technique of intimidation very successfully in South Carolina, and he was repeatedly sent to the Senate. Can you imagine that he actually spoke in support of lynch mobs organized against Blacks and supported a South Carolina Constitution of 1895 that effectively prevented Blacks from voting? Nothing is far-fetched when you think of the motivations of a demagogue. They will do or say anything to get elected.

Trump, the modern American demagogue, encouraged physical intimidation to demonstrate his strength to the masses at his rallies. He would provoke the hecklers and demonstrators for the entertainment and arousal of his followers, who on occasion assaulted some of the anti-Trump people.

All of this theater played into the hands of the demagogue, who told his supporters that they had to defend him because these people wanted to prevent him from being elected, although he knew that the elections were rigged.

Trump does not have the ability to make a discursive argument or a long discourse on any policy issue. He is a tweeter who apparently has a short span of attention and seeks other ways of conveying messages rather than policy statements. Trump uses insult and ridicule as a way to shorten deliberation. If he does not use narcissistic praise in a meeting, then he uses ridicule of people, plans, and policies. There is no discussion in detail of what the plans or policies mean to the people. Trump is rather about the show and not about the policy; in effect, policy is made by tweets. He is the first demagogue to use tweets to keep his followers attuned to his antics. At his rallies with mostly unsophisticated audiences, he is able to shout down reasoned arguments with assaults, threats, and intimidation or ridicule and shaming.

The infamous "Pitchfork" Tillman, for example, got his nickname from a speech in which he called President Grover Cleveland nothing but "an old bag of beef" and said he would bring a pitchfork to Washington to poke him in his old, fat ribs. The people laughed whenever he gave that line, and soon they started calling him by the name "Pitchfork Ben."

Trump has mastered the vulgarity and vileness of the lowest type of person in his public and private conversations. Devoid of a real passion for truth, goodness, and justice, he practices a feigned caring by resorting to platitudes and sentimentalities in the gravest situations. Name-calling, as we have seen, is one of his favorite habits. He reminds me of the reports of Vardaman, the skilled demagogue, who once called Roosevelt "a coon-flavored miscegenationist."[5] What could have compelled Vardaman to post an advertisement for "sixteen big, fat, mellow, rancid coons" to sleep in the bed with Roosevelt when he visited Mississippi? His antipathy against Blacks was known to all Mississippians, but any white who was fair and just toward African Americans also came under his glare and fire.

---

[5]William F. Holmes, *The White Chief: James Kimble Vardaman*. Baton Rouge: Louisiana State University Press, 1970.

Trump's demagoguery in the face of immigration is similar to Vardaman's with regard to Black people. Any progressive white politician, in Trump's narrow classification, a Democrat or a maverick Republican, would be attacked. As we know, Trump enjoyed creating insulting epithets for opponents as a way to keep the public from considering serious matters by diverting their attention to laughter. Personal invective against an opponent may help gain a few points for humor but does nothing to create rational discourse.

In many ways, Trump has shown a contempt for women, making them the object of ridicule, calling them names if they accused him of sexual harassment, and denying that he or his friends ever assaulted women. The dignity of women is not in his vocabulary. The verbal assault against Congresswoman Fredericka Williams by Trump and his chief of staff John Kelly was one of the most despicable examples of a demagogue's bag of tricks. They insulted her by telling a lie, and even after the news media had revealed a video that showed it was a lie, they held on to the lie and never apologized to the Congressperson. This was so blatant and so bold as to cause even those who tried to protect Trump's administration to encourage them to retract their statements and apologize to the Congressperson. Of course, here we see that a liar who holds on to a lie when it has been shown to be a lie is neither iconic nor peculiar; this liar is of the same corrupt substance and essence as the worst American demagogues.

THE DEMAGOGUE'S PROTOCOL

I think that what we have seen with Trump is that he is a disrupter, not a builder. He destroys rules, but without rules, you cannot create anything of substance. Trump has violated the basic protocols of diplomacy, collegiality, government, and personal style. He insulted a Gold Star family, that is, a family whose son had fought as an American in a war and lost his life in battle. He threatened to jail his political rivals and encouraged his followers to expect violence and to be prepared to dish out violence as well. He once pointedly told Hillary Clinton that if he became president he would get "officers to look into your situation." A third-rate threat on an opponent should be beneath American politicians, but

Trump, as a demagogue, has often seen security officers and other government officials as people who serve him personally rather than the nation. He violates all protocol to go after his opponents and critics in a negative way by insisting that the officers of government serve him. This is the radical position in which the country found itself as Trump signaled the decline of discourse and the ascendancy of bombast in political rhetoric.

HOW DEMOCRACIES DIE

Democracies are placed on the path toward death when the political leaders are corrupt and incompetent. Trump's promise to hire "the best people" turned into a farce with a cadre of losers such as Michael Flynn, Paul Manafort, Rob Porter, John Kelly, Carter Page, Rick Gates, George Papadopoulos, and nearly 130 people serving in the White House without being able to pass the full security clearing more than a year after Trump's election.

Western democracies probably learned decorum and protocol from the French professional civil class. One could, of course, trace the origin of *respect* in government to the ancient African concept of *maat*, which meant harmony, order, and balance within the context of dignity-affirming words.[6] Trump has violated many of the most sober standards established in the long history of democracies. The aim of standards, rules of political speech, and good manners is to create conditions for less emotionalism and more deliberation. However, when you have individuals who are not readers of theory, information, or literature, you tend to get the pedestrian vulgarities of Trump's athletic clubhouse.

Trump's vile language most likely comes from vulgar thoughts. He claims that his talk is the way "men talk in the locker room," but he lies; it is the way he talks wherever he is because he violates all standards of good behavior. While he may think that he is thumbing his nose at traditional

---

[6] Maulana Karenga, *Selections From the Husia*. Los Angeles, CA: University of Sankore, 1989.

politicians, he is really demonstrating that he is ignorant of the basic standards of presidential decorum. Obama, for example, elevated the office by seeking to express the elegance that should flow from the top person in the U.S. government.

The problem with Trump's lack of integrity is that he cannot help himself. He lied and placed around him others who would lie to him and give him the praise that he craved. Whatever the lengths it took him to go for praise, he would travel that distance to make himself the dominant personality in the room. He would lie often and without any reservations. Like other demagogues, Trump mastered the technique of the audacious act. He would shock those who attended his rallies with outlandish lies, tell lies to reporters about Obama wire-tapping his home, and even lie about ordinary things such as his financial condition or his tax filings. Trump is a man without restraint who is shameless in his search for attention from all sectors of the society. Because he had been in the media, he knew how to get press coverage, and he manipulated the spectacle-seeking reporters who were hungry for news, feeding them stories with dubious reasoning. He became a metrics man, measuring his numbers against those of his opponents. This is why he had his media people lie that his inauguration crowd was the largest ever, which it was not.

Aristotle is said to have written that the demagogue Cleon shouted on the public platform and used abusive language. When I read Aristotle's description of Cleon, it was a further indication that demagogues have neither style nor substance and have not changed over the years.

ONE AMONG THE MASSES

Even with his billions, Trump works on the emotions of his audiences, using the plural pronoun "we" as if he is a part of the same group as his followers. This is a common tactic demagogues use. By using this type of language, Trump drags his followers into the circle of villainy that is a part of his career.

It reminds me of the demagogue governor of Georgia, Eugene Talmadge's decoration of the Executive Mansion grounds with a barn and a henhouse to show that he was just like his voters. Trump tells the West Virginia coal miners that he is going to bring back their old mines.

This slick Manhattan businessperson convinces many ordinary people that he is one of them. Like Talmadge, Trump had speeches for different groups of people. He often spoke to veterans and farmers as though he could and would do for them what others could not or would not do. Talmadge spoke to the ordinary people who were his followers by railing against "nigger-lovin' furriners."

Trump's response to the modern world is the most backward of any recent president. He is anti-immigrant, anti-Muslim, antiscience, antitechnology, and antiknowledge. Having such attitudes means that he is capable of making complex issues appear quite simple—whether this is a matter of his own incompetence or a stroke of genius in bending the complexities of climate science, for example, into a simple Trumpism like "I think we have a cold winter, so there is no climate warming."

Many political, technological, and social issues require patience and serious contemplation, which means definition and analysis before action. The assertion that anything that poses a problem to American democracy can be negotiated with some notion of the art of the deal is quite sophomoric. Such oversimplification of complex problems imperils the nation because it demonstrates the naiveté of the president.

There are several rules followed by all demagogues. The first rule is that they have to attack the rule of law. Considering themselves above the law and outside of the political class, and holding mandates to change the rules, demagogues seek to make exceptions to rules that constrict and restrict their actions. Trump is no exception to this. He has sought to deal with his chief of staff as a creature of his own making and to put his media spokesperson in an unfortunate position where that person has to lie in order to keep that position. In this way, the people in media positions are given no choice but to defend a fuzzy line between that which is real and alternative realities. Breaking rules is often the result of not knowing the rules or refusing to accept them as applicable to your actions. Trump likes to say, "I hereby demand," as though he is asserting real power and showing that he is in charge, but his rhetoric rings hollow because of the many transgressions that he has made in the area of protocol. I am sure that as a demagogue he believes that it is unnecessary for him to study the history of American institutions, the protocols of diplomacy, and the ways of governing. You do not bark commands or demands at other citizens in a democracy; each person has rights that cannot be taken away by the president, and presidents are not above the law.

Trump's pattern is to claim that the ends justify the means. When he sets his mind on a goal, he will do anything to reach that goal. This means that he will lie and ridicule people to justify the means. Trump's mentality is much like that of other demagogues: "Only I can fix it." The demagogue will not relinquish his attachment to his exceptional qualities.

SHIFTING POSITIONS

Trump flip-flops on many ideas. *The Washington Post* of January 10, 2018, tracked the flip-flops of Trump. During the campaign of 2016, Trump said that the unemployment rate was really 42 percent and that the official statistics were false; later, he told his audiences that the unemployment rate was the lowest in seventeen years, but the truth is that the rate was already 4.6, the lowest in a decade.

An astonishing 91 times, Trump celebrated the upward swing in the stock market during his administration, yet during the presidential campaign, as the market rose under President Obama, he said that it was a bubble that would soon burst as the Federal Reserve started raising interest rates. The Fed has raised the rates at least four times since Trump was elected, and yet the stock market has not plunged. The rise in stock prices that began under Obama in 2009 continued until 2018. Rejecting all conventions of ethics, from any tradition of religion or morality, Trump refused to apologize, admit that he was wrong, or compliment the Obama administration. Instead, he went on to attack his predecessor in office and condemn the media for not supporting the Trump agenda.

Attacking the News Media

Since information from the legitimate press, where journalists double-check information, can undermine the demagogue's spell over his followers, modern demagogues have often attacked the press intemperately, calling for violence against media persons who opposed them and claiming that the press was secretly in the service of moneyed interests or foreign powers or that leading newspapers were simply out to get them. Huey Long accused the New Orleans *Times–Picayune* and the *Item* of being "bought" and asked his bodyguards to beat up their reporters. Oklahoma governor "Alfalfa Bill" Murray (1869–1956) once called for bombing the offices of the *Daily Oklahoman*. Senator Joe McCarthy declared that *The Christian Science Monitor*, the *New York Post*, *The New York Times*, the *New York Herald Tribune*, *The Washington Post*, the *St. Louis Post-Dispatch*, and many other leading American newspapers were "communist smear sheets" under the control of Moscow.

The central feature of the practice of demagoguery is persuasion by means of fearmongering shutting down reasoned deliberation and any consideration of alternatives. Demagogues pander to raw emotions, racism, prejudices, bigotry, and unreason. Indeed "McCarthyism" was coined in 1950 to describe a kind of reckless, unsubstantiated, smear type of rhetoric. All one has to do to understand Trump is to review the methods of persuasion used by most demagogues throughout history. Demagogues usually start by lying and then attacking the press. This was definitely the modus operandi under the Trump regime, where if the demagogue cannot control the media or play the media for fools, he will attack the press or simply use "alternative facts" on his own Twitter account.

MCCAIN'S LONE REPUBLICAN COUNTER TO TRUMP'S ATTACK ON THE MEDIA

"President Donald Trump's assault on the press, most often through barbed tweets and harsh words, has manifested itself more dangerously around the world," Arizona senator John McCain wrote in a *Washington Post* op-ed.[7] McCain went on to say that "reporters around the world face intimidation, threats of violence, harassment, persecution and sometimes even death as governments resort to brutal censorship to silence the truth."[8]

---

[7]John McCain wrote an op-ed in the *Washington Post* on January 16, 2017, with the title "Mr. President, Stop Attacking the Press." In the article, McCain wrote, "Whether Trump knows it or not, these efforts are being closely watched by foreign leaders who are already using his words as cover as they silence and shutter one of the key pillars of democracy."

[8]The entire McCain op-ed in *The Washington Post* (January 16, 2017) should be read.

The attitude Trump displays toward the media is unworthy of a president of a free people whose freedom is rooted in the ability to express views contrary to those of the president. Thus, one cannot simply say that Trump is hypocritical when in fact it may be a case of an individual who has no sense of appreciation for other humans. It appears that the only function Trump sees for other people is to serve his own ego. I believe this is the reason Trump continues his unrelenting assaults on American journalists.

McCain cited statistics from the Committee to Protect Journalists that 262 reporters were jailed in 2017. McCain also quoted the committee's figure of 21 reporters imprisoned the previous year on charges of "fake news," the phrase used by Trump to degrade reporting that he believes is against him.

THE SPECIAL EFFECT OF DEMAGOGIC RACISM

The issue with demagogues and their irrationality is that they distort logic and truth and also stir up the masses and sow deep divisions in society with lies. The tendency to black-and-white thinking and the hostile rhetoric toward the "other" that they encourage are damaging to the fabric of society and to critical thought.

Nevertheless, demagogues have been a societal staple since ancient times. Wherever there are segments of society that can be riled up, there will be demagogues. Well-known demagogues include Huey P. Long, Joseph McCarthy, and Father Charles Coughlin, a forerunner of the modern talk show radio hosts. A review of other historical figures who have earned the label of "demagogue" shows us convincingly that Trump is not an aberration in American society, although one hopes that he is an aberration in the presidency.

A Parade of Political Hooligans

Theodore Bilbo was Mississippi's most dominant personality during the first quarter of the twentieth century. Bilbo was a segregationist with a fiery spirit and an extravagant attitude who believed that Blacks were an idle and slothful people. There was nothing in Bilbo but hatred for

Africans, who he saw as subhuman. Bilbo's rudeness made him notorious for his lack of civility, but he believed that the "general feeling" of whites was with him. His contemporaries called him a strutting peacock although his height was just 5 feet 5 inches.

As a demagogue, Bilbo expressed contempt for Blacks whenever he could to gain credibility with poor whites. The use of the poor and uneducated white population is a cardinal principle of American demaguery. The idea is to invest in the poor and uneducated whites with the powerful privilege of skin royalty by making them the inheritors of the dream of a white nation with other people whose purpose is to serve whiteness. As attractive as this dream might be to some whites, especially those who saw Trump as a kind of white knight, it is an impossible reality.

Since the turn of the twentieth century, the United States has embraced the vision of a nation seeking to enable all of its citizens and others with the democratic meme. Of course, this was contrary to the political ideology adhered to by Bilbo, and as a result, the nation found itself torn between race wars and racial reconciliation for decades. Yet, thrust into the national rhetoric by Africans, women, and labor unions, the idea of diversity took hold and became a leading tendency in the latter half of the twentieth century. This particular characterization of the nation gave birth to the progressive sentiments that challenged the neoliberal and conservative traditions that have always found their way into American discourse. Thus, Bilbo represented the reactive thrust, the element of radical nationalism based on race, class, and a search for the status quo ante.

Bilbo said that his opponents were corrupters of southern womanhood, and skunks who stole Gideon Bibles from hotel rooms. He told the people that he knew there were many communists in the government and so the people should elect him to clean it up. This is reminiscent of Trump's promise to "drain the swamp."

Demagogues always seem to know more than other people because they lie more easily than others and do not have a penchant for research or facts. The fact that Bilbo went around speaking about communists in the government without ever citing any evidence opened the door for Joseph McCarthy to walk down the same stench-filled corridor nearly twenty-five years later. Trump would later take up the cry of the "deep state" as he was

unable to speak about communists since the reports stated that his government had extremely close, even criminal, contacts with Putin's Russia.

When Bilbo entered the Senate, he railed against Africans. He was a
vicious attacker of Blacks and introduced bizarre bills that were meant
to resettle Blacks in West Africa. He once demanded that all Africans
should be moved out of Washington, D.C.). As head of the Senate
Committee with oversight of the District of Columbia, Bilbo sought to
stop the increase in the number of Blacks moving into the district. In fact,
he was adamant that there were too many Black people in the city, and
they had to move. Of course, the city's population prevailed, and the
Black people remained in the city long after Bilbo had left it.

Like all demagogues, Bilbo knew that his vile language and coarse style
would draw some followers. There was segregation in Washington in the
1940s, and Bilbo made sure that the people did not forget that it was a
southern city despite his inability to evacuate all the Blacks.

Trump also borrows from Lewis Charles Levin, a crusader, as he called
himself, obsessed with the idea of getting rid of all aliens who were cor-
rupting America. Immigration, so often seen as a part of the genius of
America and a pillar of the diversity that marked the United States as
different from European nations, became a rod to poke in the sides of the
emotional body of Trump supporters. He defied the established virtue of
seeking more diversity and more unique gifts that constituted America's
special quality and substituted it with a bitter anger against all immigration. Trump started his assault on the Mexicans and then on the
Dreamers, the children who were brought to the United States by their
parents, who were raised in the United States, served in the army, went
to college, and worked as Americans. They were anathema to his narrow
white right-wing ideology. He rolled back the executive order that had
been made by Obama providing a pathway to normalizing the residency
of the Dreamers. Trump declared a deadline for them to leave the country
by March 2018, even though the only home they knew was the United
States. Not only was this position irrational, but it was also cruel and
mean-spirited. Through no fault of their own, the Dreamers lived in the
United States and served their country, and they signed up to give their
names and addresses in order to be legitimate only to find that Trump
would exploit their information to try to expel them from their country.

Trump's demagoguery reveals that his anti-immigration stand is against all foreigners, not just the Dreamers. He has sought to change even "legal" immigration to limit the number of people coming from Africa, Asia, Latin America, and the Caribbean. He expressed his anger at the immigration of Haitians and Africans from "shithole nations," asking his Republican colleagues and aides, in the presence of Democrats, why America couldn't get "more Norwegians."

One is apt to think that this type of behavior is uncharacteristic of a president of the United States, but Trump has changed the equations of decency by succumbing to the most negative aspects of the American personality: selfishness, hegemony, racism, and a willingness to degrade any person who does not think or act like he does.

Lewis Charles Levin foreshadowed Trump with his self-styled crusader persona by cursing at those who were considered aliens. His single idea was the protection of white Protestant culture against the "danger of subversion by the influx of that horde of aliens, who combine to break down its barriers, that they may command in the citadel, or overrun the land." Perhaps those who give their support to Trump have forgotten that the Irish, the Italians, and the Greeks could not have held their place in Levin's cultural war. He did not care if they were legal or undocumented; he simply did not want them to defile the America he knew. For Trump, the idea is to keep out those who are not white and to bring in only those who increase the numbers of the white community. This is a demagoguery based on the fear of the other. Levin's declared enemy was Roman Catholicism, which he believed to be an organization of "alien" European criminals.

Levin was the son of Jewish parents, born in Charleston, South Carolina, in 1808, when the white enslavement of Africans was at its peak. In the year of his birth, the Constitution ended the importation of Africans for the purpose of slavery. However, the sentiment in the slaveholding South was anti-African. Levin grew up in this environment in South Carolina and would later attack immigrants from Europe. Some people believe that Levin felt some cultural alienation himself and this caused him to rant against Roman Catholics. After he was wounded in a duel in the South, Levin settled in Philadelphia, Pennsylvania, and became the editor of *The Temperance Advocate*.

At the age of 51, he sold *The Temperance Advocate* and purchased the *Daily Sun*, which he used to advance his obsession with the country's growing Irish Catholic population. A major conspiracy theorist, Levin believed that the Roman Catholic Church was trying to conquer the United States by bringing more Irish people to overwhelm the election process.

When Levin held a campaign meeting on May 3, 1844, in Kensington, just north of downtown Philadelphia, a mob gathered outside to attack him for his insulting remarks about Irish people. Levin retaliated by threatening to burn down St. Michael's Church. Subsequently, Levin's group, calling themselves the Nativists, held another rally after three days with his followers armed with guns. When an argument occurred between an Irishman and a Nativist, it led to several days of riots in Philadelphia in which the Nativists sought to burn down every Catholic church in the city. This anti-immigrant attitude was latent in American society, and it took the demagogue Levin to resurrect it with his vile rhetoric of hate.

After the riots, the demagogue Levin rode the wave of anti-Catholicism all the way to getting elected to Congress, in which he served from 1845 to 1851. His speech to the House of Representatives in 1848 is one of the vilest antireligious speeches ever made against Catholics in the Congress. His obsession with foreigners, especially Catholics, bordered on irrational fear, and at the end of his life, some speculate that his bitterness may have driven him to insanity and death. What we see in the Trump era is that the descendants of some of the people who were attacked in the past for being foreigners are now the same people who today attack others. How is it that Catholics, Italians, Jews, Poles, and Irish support the older, vile rhetoric produced by those who claimed that the country belonged to them alone? Do they not remember their own history? This shows us that a demagogue can use any group as the out-group and can get people to accept hatred against that out-group with an emotional rhetoric for political gain.

THE UBIQUITOUS NATURE OF DEMAGOGUES

The United States is not the only country to have demagogues. Udo Voigt, the German politician, who has served since 2014 in the

European Parliament, once called Hitler "a great German statesman," causing consternation among many Europeans. Voigt thought that the Nazi Rudolf Hess should be nominated for the Nobel Peace Prize. Voigt's personal style might be called that of an individual shock trooper who sought to stir up the public with his wild pronouncements.

Most demagogues claim that they are the only ones with the answers for the masses. Voigt, for example, called for an armed uprising against the government of Germany in 1998 because he believed that the country was occupied by outsiders and anti-Germans, and he was the only clear-eyed German to see the problem. Reaching out to the United States, he made contact with white racists, including David Duke, the former Ku Klux Klan wizard and an anti-Semite. Duke called Voigt the "true chancellor of Germany."

Demagogues tell lies at any time and at any place with no difficulty. Voigt, for instance, said, in contradiction to the historically accepted death count of six million Jews in the Holocaust, that the number was only 340,000. Udo Pastoers, a German racist who followed the example of Voigt's rhetoric, was charged with inciting racial hatred, which is a crime in Germany, for calling Germany a "Jew Republic" and calling the Turkish minority "semen cannons." Like Trump, the German demagogues isolated groups of people who they thought should be denied something that others, mainly white Christians, were entitled to have.

Trump is morally corrupt, but he is not politically inept because the lies that make him immoral have served to advance his cause with his followers. When they support him, it looks like they believe that he can tell no lies, and they serve as his brick wall of protection from the spotlight of reason.

I find it difficult to understand those who believe Trump's lie that he has been "tougher on Russia than Obama" given the fact that while Trump, for more than a year, refused to impose the sanctions on Russia that were voted by Congress., Obama actually expelled 35 Russians, took control of two of their properties, imposed sanctions on the country, and told President Putin to "cut it out" during the last months of his second term.

Trump's demagoguery borders on psychopathic reasoning. It reminds me of the logic finessed by the racists in eighteenth century Pennsylvania who wanted to deny free Blacks the right to vote. They argued in court that although those Africans seeking to vote were free, "being free negroes is not the same as free men"; therefore, free Blacks could not be allowed to vote because they were not free men. Racism creates not just distortions of truth but also the most bizarre contortions of reason.

DEFENDING THE PROCESS FROM DISRUPTION

Trump's acrimonious rhetoric and chaotic administration underline his attacks on the democratic process. It looks like the president came into office from the streets with no obvious familiarity with the Constitution, political protocols, or the consultative realities of the political process. Like a child who cries when he cannot get his way, Trump not only cries but also seeks to destroy what he cannot comprehend. The Trump phenomenon corrupts ordinary conversation and renders rational argument and discourse mute in preference to shouts of "You are fired!" It is as if Trump's doggedly pessimistic attitude toward the truth, facts, and logic imperils every sector of society.

One sees boldness in the white supremacist community because Trump has made white supremacy popular among some people who may have been latent racists. They want to be like him, to have money and power, and to dominate others with commands and demands of the oddest kind. This sickness is seen in the world of sports teams, on the playgrounds of urban communities, and in the circles of wealth and status in major cities, where people dish out and receive insults as if these are the calling cards of relationships.

Charlottesville was Trump's opportunity to demonstrate leadership, but he demonstrated his waffling on the issue of bigotry. When neo-Nazis, white supremacists, and bigots marched in Charlottesville, Virginia, to protest the removal of Confederate statues representing the supporters of the rebellion against the Union and to support the men who fought to preserve slavery, Trump choked and came up very short in his remarks. It was August 2017, and hundreds of chanting white supremacists yelled hateful words, and one of them, James Alex Fields Jr., plowed his Dodge Challenger into a crowd of counterprotesters, killing Heather Heyer, 32, of Charlottesville and wounding 19 other people.

On August 16, 2017, Trump said, among other things, that there were good and bad people on both sides. A firestorm of protest against his comments erupted when he said to the reporters, "I think there is blame on both sides." He declared, "There are fine people on both sides." Was he mad? How could a president be so detached from history and reality that he did not understand that moment? Perhaps, he understood that moment precisely and was happy to roll back the nation's discourse to racial epithets and deep resentments. It was a sad statement, but it was one that we had come to expect from Trump. There was nothing aspirational in his spirit; his sentiment was stale, antiquated, boring, and unforgivable.

CONFRONTING THE DEMAGOGUE

So what must be done? The antidote to demagoguery is always the truth. I feel that the American public has been served well by the mainstream media, which has held Trump responsible for the lies that he has told from the comfort of the Oval Office, Mar-a-Lago, or his Manhattan penthouse. Surrounded by white nationalists like Steve Bannon and Steve Miller during his first year and those who lie for him, like Sarah Huckabee Sanders, Kellyanne Conway, and Raj Shah, Trump fired his cannons of lies every day in an effort to flood the airwaves with chaos. Only the Fourth Estate has challenged him in his own arena, the public platform. In Trump's first year in office, when things were unraveling, Republican leaders in Congress refused to rein him in; indeed, some of them appeared to serve as Trump's stooges, like Representative Devin Nunes, although he was leading the House committee investigating the Russian interference in the election of 2016.

Free people must exercise liberty, or they will see it evaporate into thin air. The degrading of public discourse precedes the degrading of public trust and thrusts the nation into an existential travesty. Therefore, all conscious citizens should step forward to declare themselves as defenders of the democratic compact that makes us Americans. The only way we know that we are free is when we are able to make such declarations without duress.

Let us be clear about the real meaning of Donald Trump, his origin and support base beyond what is obvious and conceded. Trump did not come into being by himself or remain in place by himself. He does not live, thrive, and spew anti-Mexican and anti-Muslim toxic lines without active and latent supporters. Many of the marchers at Charlottesville shouted, "*Weise Menschen uber alles*" ("White people over all") and "Jews will not replace us!"

Our response must condemn the vulgar bigotry that defies humanity and makes this nation a repository of "unfreedom." Our act of goodwill must begin with us renouncing those who count blood more important than community. Therefore, we cannot sanction any form of demagoguery, and we must not open the door to anti-African, anti-Muslim, anti-Semitic, and homophobic rhetoric. We must be antiracist, anticorporatist, and antisexist to regain our pace toward genuine liberation. Let us reject all political stupidity and low-life rhetoric that create insanity in our society. Acceptance of the humanity of the other is the definition of our own humanity. Who will explain why racism is morally wrong? Who will pursue the mean-spirited demagogues and chase them out of the temples? It can only be us; we are the ones we are looking out for, and once we accept the challenge, the demagogues will have met their match.

Only when we see that values are more important than votes and that being good people is better than being rich people can we overcome the weakness that causes us to believe, at times, that because a person has money, he or she also has goodness. What I learned from the people's election of Trump, with Russia's assistance, is that the fragility of our society is hanging by the thread of our ethical imagination. Without ethics, we are no more than odd political pawns in the game of elections, however frequently they are held. To assert ourselves as champions of an authentic community means that we will have to undergo criticism, but we will resist Trump and other demagogues who seek to steal our liberation. No single-issue litmus test candidate should be allowed to "trump" profound discourses about the good of society. Trump will always support inordinate wealth grabbing, domination through bullying, deprivation of health care, and the power of the gun industry parading as NRA (National Rifle Association) membership. On the other hand, we are stronger than evil and more resilient than the last grand demagogue who thinks that his messianic vision is the one that we should sign on to, but alas, we are merely tough, unadulterated warriors for the truth.

THE DEMAGOGUE AS THE BURNING MAN

Trump rose to the top of the Republican primary battle for the 2016 election by taking his populist appeal seriously to the largely white Republican Party and attacking every institution and personality that stood in his way. As a declared businessperson and reality television personality, Trump used his popularity to slash through his Republican opponents. Jeb Bush, Marco Rubio, Ted Cruz, and John Kasich were the main targets of Trump's barbs, outlandish remarks, and character and personality attacks. His obloquy had no limits as he aimed to destroy his opposition in the media. The violence of his thoughts that was reflected in his vile language meant that the demagogue had no power of reflection; he personified impulsive action, almost without a pause.

Trump promised his audiences that he would return America to greatness by keeping out immigrants from poor countries out, reducing taxes on the wealthy, and demonstrating his negotiation tactics in dealing with adversaries. His demagoguery was fervent, constant, and hostile toward all the groups that he felt were easy targets for his followers. He attacked Mexicans and Muslims, promising to build a wall on the border with Mexico and then banning Muslims from entering the country. His rhetoric against women was seen as offensive by most of the nation. He also disparaged the character of Senator John McCain and impugned the character of the father of an American soldier who was killed in combat. Regarding McCain, who had earlier run for the presidency on the Republican ticket, Trump declared that he did not like soldiers who were captured like McCain was during the Vietnam War. McCain was and is widely considered an American hero. Meanwhile, Trump, with no military experience, casts himself among his followers as the wisest of military leaders. Clearly, he takes his audience on a fool's errand, and he knows that they do not care so long as he stokes their fears of the progressives and the boogeyman deep state, which does not exist anymore than the Illuminati that is believed to run the world.

Trump ran against Hillary Clinton and won the presidency, although she won more popular votes. Trump picked up more electoral college votes and therefore won the presidency, to the dismay of many progressive people, especially women who had wanted to see the first woman president.

He did it, as a demagogue would do, by slamming her with lies, creating false narratives of her "lack of stamina," and seeking to intimidate her in debates. She was sharper, more intelligent, and more experienced, but what Trump proved was that none of that matters when the population wants the red meat of white racial nationalism.

Never had a contest for the presidency of the United States brought two people together who were more unlike. Hillary Clinton was a U.S. Senator for New York, she had been the First Lady of the United States, and she had served as secretary of state under Obama. Her experience was phenomenal. On the other hand, Trump had no government experience and was perceived by expert political observers as a weak candidate when it came to policies, ethics, and experience. What Trump had was a demeaning attitude toward his audience. A billionaire, so he claimed, but one who understood the lives of the poor religious white southerners and midwesterners more than anyone else? What he believed was that the white masses were "stupid" enough to accept a New York billionaire's appeal to their racist ideas of white supremacy. Some people shook their heads in disbelief because they could not believe that Trump could appeal to people who were so unlike him. But the demagogue knows human psychology, that it does not matter where the demagogue is born or resides; using the provocative language of race and racial superiority seems to have captured even the God-fearing, bible-thumping preachers of the Christian Church.

The Republicans led a vicious attack on Hillary Clinton, claiming that she was untrustworthy because of her use of a private server for official emails during the time she was secretary of state. Trump used that to launch an assault on Clinton's character, something that she refused to do about Trump's character. He led his audiences on shouts of "Lock her up! Lock her up!"—and soon people began to rate her negatively. Clinton was never found guilty of anything illegal, but Trump's attacks had their sting and caused Clinton to lose the election by a few votes.

The television program *Access Hollywood* revealed that Trump had boasted about his sexual exploits with women in 2005, showing predatory behavior by the man who would be president. Trump said it was just "locker room talk," but some women decided that they could not vote for him on the basis of his behavior. Nevertheless, Clinton was not able to overcome the handicap handed to her by the questions about the private email server. Although she beat Trump by 2.8 million votes, he gathered the minimum 270 electoral college votes needed in the critical states to allow him to become president. Each state is awarded a certain number of electoral votes, and when those votes are cast based on who the people in that state voted for, they are counted and the person with 270 electoral votes wins. Therefore, although Clinton won California with a lead of more than 4 million votes over Trump, California could only count its electoral votes, not its popular votes, in the final tally.

The day after Trump's inauguration in 2016, the Women's Marches brought millions of people to the streets. They feared a White House that would use the idea of a nationalist politic to punish people, deny human rights, and trample on the equality of women. There were not enough fact-checkers of Trump's speeches to counter the lies he told. He brought controversy everywhere he turned. Nothing familiar seemed to stand in its place. He used social media regularly to make policy. He termed the news from established companies as "fake" news, claiming that he and his allies were the only real voices providing real news.

As a demagogue without shame, Trump took on the role of defining the narrative of the country in his own image, minimizing all the structures of government and micromanaging the work of many departments, some of which did not have permanent leadership during Trump's administration.

A democracy is built on generations of agreements, relationships with other nations, intergovernmental activities, and trust. A demagogue will never permit such regular business; his main aim is to disrupt and to interrupt. Thus, he tried to destroy Obamacare, end the Trans-Pacific Partnership, counteract Obama's policies on the environment, reopen the Keystone XL Pipeline discussion, and withdraw from the Paris Climate Agreement. He also reiterated his aim to build a massive wall between the United States and Mexico and make Mexico pay for it.

Employing the same bombast internationally, Trump found saber-rattling language to counter Kim Jong-Un's North Korean rhetoric. Both men jockeyed for position on a wide range of military issues with threats of fiery fury.

Trump's administration was in turmoil from the beginning. Steve Bannon was fired; Michael Flynn was forced out for lying to Vice President Pence about a meeting with Sergy Kislyak, the Russian ambassador to the United States, Jeff Sessions was terminated as attorney general, and James Comey of the FBI was fired. Scores of lower-level employees left the administration because they could no longer stomach such disorganization and chaos in government. But what can we expect when the leader of the nation is an avowed narcissist? We should look for the symptoms of a maladjusted adolescent seeking to run all other bicycles out of the lane for two-wheelers.

There are no ethics and no redemption in narcissism. Those who put on the cloak of the demagogue, for whatever reason, do so only in their interest, and there are no other objectives, aims, or goals. Demagogues and dictators are not necessarily the same type of people. However, if the demagogue exists in a dictator, then the society will suffer in ways that are immeasurable.

By the grace of its institutions, the United States survived the first coming of Donald Trump. These institutions, especially the state and federal courts, are our last best chance for checking the power of a demagogue who would be, in his own words, a dictator if he ever became president of the United States again.

CHAPTER 6
Bending Away From the Ridiculous

Donald Trump's name will live in infamy, to paraphrase Franklin Roosevelt's statement about the bombing of Pearl Harbor.

Trump broke the back of the American myth of exclusivity when it came to the sacrosanct issue of presidential succession after an election. Never in the history of the United States of America, under the Constitution, had a president sought to retain the office after the election.

There was no guise to Trump's dastardly attempt to subvert the election by trying to force Vice President Mike Pence to halt the certification of the vote and to replace the authentic electors with fake electors.

Political gall, pure and simple, was Trump's call to notoriety. He flaunted and falsified every statute and every rule of order that he saw right from the first days of being in the office of president.

Trump darkened the light of democracy, bringing to bear on the American system of democracy the most primitive elements of power-hungry demagogues, whose only ambition is to run roughshod over all accepted and acceptable norms.

In effect, Trump, like most demagogues, was enamored with his own image. He had found at an early age that he could bully, harass, and push others to limits that were unknown in most social and political venues. He was the exceptional man, willing to explore the boundaries of ethics, values, and dogma. He saw himself as the frontage road to every opportunity to show power, prestige, and money. No wonder, he had wanted to build the tallest hotel in the center of Moscow. No wonder that he loved President Vladimir Putin and President Xi, while he hated Hillary Clinton, Barack Obama, and Joe Biden. Demagogues love other demagogues because they believe that no one understands them except other people with the same ambitions.

Trump harbored a loathing for the public. In this respect, he was no different from other demagogues who believed that the masses of people in a society would believe anything, accept any policy, and vote against their own interests if you are able to convince them with big lies.

I was initially worried when journalists began identifying Trump as a natural liar during the first weeks of his campaign for the 2016 election. Others were amazed as they tried to understand how a person could tell such bold lies with impunity. Trump did it, and I knew that it meant he would follow the pattern of the European demagogues whose names are etched in history, such as Adolf Hitler, Benito Mussolini, and Franco. The Countries like Germany, Italy, and Spain, considered forward thinking, had at one time or the other seen demagogues who used lies to bring their masses to destruction. Susceptibility to demagoguery is not a measure of culture or civilization. What it means is that most people in a society are willing to give up their ability to reason for the sake of religion.

It is hard to see how this works if you are not familiar with the conspiracy theories, lies, and falsifications of reality used in the devilish quest to acquire power.

The demagogue, as in the case of Trump, identifies with the masses using a vile, blood-and-soil approach that is directly opposite to modernity and postmodernity. It is, at its core, a racist ideology parading as a political strategy, when it is actually a religion based on the idea that "others" are trying to "replace" the real people of blood. It is an antihuman movement, full of the venom that comes with fear and hatred, seeking to announce a mass movement of a "special" people.

In Trump's case, it was from the beginning about his German identity and his German blood and the fact that he was supposed to be really smart, smarter than most people, when the evidence of his lifestyle and actions shows that he was often very stupid. Being boastful and bragging about how intelligent you are do not make one smart. I have come to believe that Trump has an inferiority complex and that is why he feels that he has to act "big" and like he has more money, power, and fame than other people.

One of the reasons Trump attacked what he called the "deep state" is because the career employees serving in most of the government offices in Washington, D.C., are people who have dedicated their lives to the interests of bureaucratic Washington. A sizable number of these employees are African American and Latin American. They migrated to Washington to work in government jobs because the government as an employer was far more open than corporate America during the 1960s and 1970s. Trump and his Republican associates want to eliminate the Department of Education and other cabinet posts where they believe there may be too many Black employees. This is the so-called deep state that provides so much angst for demagogues.

Trump knows that a strong cadre of civil servants of all races know the laws and the Constitution and have dedicated themselves to the service of the nation. This is also one of the challenges the demagogue wishes to eradicate. The demagogue does not want to reform democracy but to destroy it because democracy stands as a barrier to the outright egoism reflected in the demagogue's personality.

There is a leaning into the people as *ethnos*, blood. The altar of the American demagogue is the racial identity of the white masses. On this altar, Trump has been able to place all the grievances of the white population. They are heavily laden with guilt, fear, and doom.

When a "strong man" comes and tells them that they are being assaulted and attacked and may even "lose their country" if they do not fight, he is mocking them. It is a form of ridicule; in fact, the demagogue is the definitive ridiculous man. He wants the grieved white masses to fight for him but not for themselves, because if they fought for themselves, they would be fighting for all Americans, Jews, Africans, immigrants, the poor, the downtrodden, the homeless, and the often-accosted transpeople, who are beaten on the streets, sometimes by those who claim to have their own grievances.

The idea of a strong man has a lot to do with a strong rhetoric, language that seeks to persuade the masses that he is tough, defiant, and invulnerable. But this is a lie; it is a weak facade, damaged every day by the fallibility of the "strong man." Ultimately, in a democratic society, it is the people who must be strong in the sense that they must always fight to keep the institutions that are the guardrails of democracy upright.

Trump is the perfect example of the ridiculous man. The trope that the "deep state" wants to harm the people who compose the state but cannot do so because "I am standing in the way" is false and ridiculous on face value.

Trump knows the truth about his weakness, but the ridiculous man cannot admit that he is scared, ordinary, and a phantom. He can do nothing that establishes himself as greater than the personal moment. He is a finite individual, just like other individuals, seeking to announce something profound but only finds the profane to his liking.

There was a time when many of us thought that by listening to his speeches, reading about his life, and discovering his immense contradictions, his core followers would "see the light" and recover from this hideous nightmare; however, the nightmare starring the ridiculous man became even more appealing as Trump became more profane.

It was his irreverence and desecration of the established institutional orthodoxies that many Evangelical and conservative Christians found appealing. The magnetism of a ruthless cavalier patriarch who regarded Africans, immigrants, and non–western European people with contempt converged with Trump's self-importance in a way that created a dangerous mixture of sacred and profane stagecraft. Those who were supposed to be Christians were, in effect, abetting the most selfish and criminally directed presidential candidate and president the American nation has had in recent times. While Trump never had a murderous track record like Andrew Jackson, who massacred Indigenous people as if they were not human and abused the Africans who he had enslaved in a brutal fashion, had he lived during the times of Jackson, he would have vied for the title of the most ridiculous.

I think Trump preferred, like most demagogues, to live outside the rules because the ridiculous man is "too big" for rules. On one occasion, Trump boasted that he did not pay taxes because "he is smart," implying that those who pay taxes are not smart.

Societies are established by conversation, not by fiat or decree, and the conversation involves other people, different opinions, engagement with the community, and respect for common principles.

Once set in motion, the principles of a society, if they are fair, can enable it to function without overseers. It has always been the case that dignity and integrity do not need rules; one either believes in and practices them, or one does not. Lasting societies are not made by dictators, and those societies that are created based on racial identities promoted by demagogues will always encounter modifications, transformations, and revolutions.

The demagogue is a ridiculous man because he fetishizes himself, eager to show that he is above all others in respect to knowledge, when in fact he is below others in terms of what he knows. Quick to tell people that he went to Wharton Business School at Penn, there is no indication that Trump distinguished himself as a student there. Rushing to claim his German blood, he has beguiled himself about many contemporary Germans, who have sought more than people from most other countries to rid themselves of the ugly stain of the Holocaust. When I spoke in Munich a few years ago, the people felt ashamed when I mentioned that we would happily send him back to Bavaria. Of course, I was trying to make a joke, but it was a poor one and did not make the audience feel proud.

Then, what is it about the 30% of white Americans who are attracted to Trump in such cult-like terms? Since the ridiculous man can never free them from their guilt and fears, why do they trust him? Since the ridiculous man is a prevaricator who quibbles about the simplest matters, why do they discover a hero in him? The ridiculous man treats women with disrespect, so why do some women adore him?

The answer to these questions brings us back to what the demagogue understands about human nature. The communication scholar Erika Vora wrote many years ago that a major social factor in separating a group from other groups of people is kinship. The belief that one group is the descendant from a set of ancestors which is different from those of any other group. . . . In terms of biological and genetic factors, the human being is like other animals. However, the human has a culture, a system of language, beliefs, activities, and ways which serve to differentiate him from all other animals.[1]

Trump leans heavily on kinship, and this is evident in his openly racist message to his followers. It is not subtle to those who understand the code language of white racial nationalism and its dangerous antecedents in the Western world.

I have always claimed that it is not a difference in kinship that creates problems; it is the idea that one particular kinship is better or worse than another. The ridiculous man argues for the superiority of his type of kinship over that of other people. The danger in this kind of rhetoric is that it stokes competitive racial ideologies that can lead to outbursts of genocide and ethnic cleansing.

The ridiculous man caters to a group of people who desire to be special. To a large degree, although claiming to be religious, they have lost faith in their divinities and now seek in the ridiculous man the mundane relics of a "glorious" past, when they were, in their minds, superior. The times of their supposed superiority existed, however, only in their minds, and even those whose bodies were stolen and held in bondage and those whose lands were stolen and who were placed on reservations never saw the white people as superior to them. Yet the ridiculous man, the demagogue par excellence, hollers louder than ever that they have been reduced to inferior beings because they have stood by and watched other people bring in more immigrants and flood universities, corporations, and communities with black, brown, and yellow people from India, Nigeria, Honduras, China, and so on. This is scapegoating of the most pernicious type where the flaws of a society are laid on the backs of people from other nations. Trump proselytizes by going to this trope every

---

[1]Erika Vora, *The Development of Concept Diffusion Models and Their Application to the Diffusion of the Social Concept of Race*. PhD Dissertation, SUNY–Buffalo, 1978.

time he feels the need to get the attention of white audiences. They respond in kind with loud shouts and yells, even clamoring to be heard, saying "USA! USA!"

One wonders what they think the United States is today. It is a multiethnic, multicultural, multireligious, and pluralistic society with people from all over the world as citizens. This is a nation of 342,000,000 people with a white population of about 58%. The number of people will continue to increase, and the percentage of whites is expected to continue to decline. The American population will become browner in the next few decades and into the future. A demagogue cannot stop this shift in population; the country will have to reaffirm its commitment to the basic institutions of a free democracy regardless of who will be the majority population in fifty years.

Hitler wrote in *Mein Kampf* that when he left Vienna in 1913 to go to Germany, he "was repelled by the conglomeration of races which the capital showed me, repelled by this whole mixture of Czechs, Poles, Hungarians, Ruthenians, Serbs, and everywhere the eternal mushroom of humanity, the Jews, everywhere the Jews."[2]

When Trump plays the "us against them" card, he is seeking to solidify an ideology based on white racial superiority to propel himself into power. It is a ridiculous man's strategy, but it finds its source in the nature of the American nation's origin.

The invasion of the North American continent by western Europeans was a relentless, brutal, and genocidal assault on the Indigenous people of this land. This is a fact not disputed by historians. The appropriation of the lands of the First Nations was an onslaught that has never completely ended, and the remaining people share lands that are some of the least fertile in the continent. They are mostly out of sight and out of mind.

Trump knows this but in his reach for personal power is willing to disregard the First Nations as if they were inferior people. His largely white audiences rally to his side because they see him as a warrior. One might

---

[2]Adolf Hitler, *Mein Kampf*. New York, NY: Reynal, 1940, p. 22.

laugh, but this is too serious for laughter; instead, we must understand that those who see him as a warrior are often blinded by their own sense of pride at a white man disrespecting other people from "shithole countries" and being irreverent when it comes to assaulting the bodies of women. One woman was heard saying, "He's a real man."

One senses that this "real man" has shown us the futility of a good education and a wealthy upbringing, both devoid of ethics and integrity. In fact, one wonders what he learned about American society along the way. Was he taught about the necessary goal it took to set up a government on a land that was occupied for millennia by another people? Did he learn about the kidnapping of Africans, their transfer to the English colonies against their will and the forcing of their descendants to work for two hundred and fifty years clearing land for farms, factories, and cities and laying railroads to connect the country? Of course, the "real Americans" have no knowledge or little knowledge of how their ancestors won the land from the Native peoples or how their ancestors raped, murdered, and mutilated the African population stolen from Africa. Furthermore, they do not want to hear it or have their children learn those lessons. They seem to prefer that their children remain dumb. In fact, Albert Camus understood precisely why "the absurd mind cannot so much expect ethical rules at the end of its reasoning," and I say that similarly the ridiculous man wants nothing more than ignorance to propel him to the top of the heap, with no regard to the broken bodies and minds of those on whom he tramples![3]

Beware of the man who claims to stand between you and the abyss; he is often the bringer of the abyss! The demagogue with the arrogant assertion of superior knowledge is more likely to be the one who is betting on the people's inability to see that the demagogue has no clothes. Our only hope is to bend the arc of democracy away from the ridiculous.

---

[3]Albert Camus, *The Myth of Sisyphus and Other Essays*. New York, NY: Vintage, 1955, p. 30.

APPENDICES
Chart 1

MAJOR AMERICAN DEMAGOGUES

Andrew Jackson (1767–1845)

President of the United States

Joseph R. McCarthy (1908–1957)

Senator of Wisconsin

Theodore Gilmore Bilbo (1877–1947)

Governor of Mississippi

"Pitchfork" Ben Tillman (1847–1918)

Governor of South Carolina

Huey "The Kingfish" Long (1893–1939)

Senator of Louisiana

Donald Trump (1946–)

President of the United States

ANDREW JACKSON (1767–1845)

President of the United States

Principal Target: Native Americans

"Andrew Jackson exhibits four attributes of demagoguery: 1. Disregard for laws and autocratic behavior; 2. Condemnation of the established government and use of outsider rhetoric; 3. Employs lies and fear tactics; and 4. Incites violence." In Andrew Hartman, "The Case Against Andrew Jackson," *U.S. Intellectual History Blog*, October 28, 2016.

JOSEPH R. MCCARTHY (1908–1957)

Senator of Wisconsin

Principal Target: Communists
Robert G. Kaiser, "Joseph McCarthy, an American Demagogue Who Foreshadowed Donald Trump," *The Washington Post*, August 27, 2020.

THEODORE GILMORE BILBO (1877–1947)

Governor of Mississippi

Principal Target: African Americans

"A demagogue and lifelong Democrat, he was a filibusterer whose name was synonymous with white supremacy. Like many Southern Democrats of his era, Bilbo believed that black people were inferior; he defended segregation, and was a member of the Ku Klux Klan, the United States' most notable white supremacist terrorist organization." See Reinhard H. Luthin, *American Demagogues*. Boston, MA: Beacon Press, 1954.

"PITCHFORK" BEN TILLMAN (1847–1918)

Governor of South Carolina

Principal Target: African Americans

Clark E. Culpepper, "Pitchfork Ben Tillman and the Emergence of Southern Demagoguery, *Quarterly Journal of Speech*, Vol. 69, November 1983, pp. 423–433.

HUEY "THE KINGFISH" LONG (1893–1939)

Senator of Louisiana

Principal Target: African Americans

Huey Long was a demagogue with dictatorial ambitions. He was known for his skillful use of language, attacks on institutions of government, and flattery of white supremacists. See John Adam Moreau, "Huey Long and His Chroniclers," *Louisiana History: The Journal of the Louisiana Historical Society*, Vol. 6, No. 2, Spring 1965, pp. 121–139.

DONALD TRUMP (1946–)

President of the United States 2017–2021

Chart 2

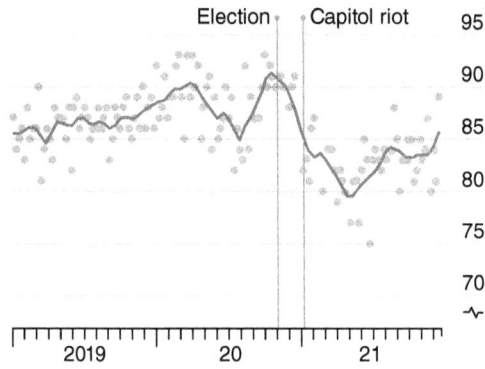

Election | Capitol riot

95
90
85
80
75
70

2019 | 20 | 21

Source: YouGov/*The Economist*

Chart 3

**Donald Trump:
"False or
misleading claims"**

Data source: *The Washington Post*

(y-axis: Monthly, 0–4,000)

**Donald Trump:
"False claims"**

Data: adapted from Daniel
Dale graphics from
Toronto Star and CNN

(y-axis: Weekly, 0–250)

(data unavailable)   (data unavailable)

x-axis: Jan '17, Apr '17, Jul '17, Oct '17, Jan '18, Apr '18, Jul '18, Oct '18, Jan '19, Apr '19, Jul '19, Oct '19, Jan '20, Apr '20, Jul '20, Oct '20, Jan '21

**Claims made by
Donald Trump**

(y-axis: Monthly, 0–4,000)

**False or
misleading**

False

Data not available

x-axis: Jan '17, Apr '17, Jul '17, Oct '17, Jan '18, Apr '18, Jul '18, Oct '18, Jan '19, Apr '19, Jul '19, Oct '19, Jan '20, Apr '20, Jul '20, Oct '20, Jan '21

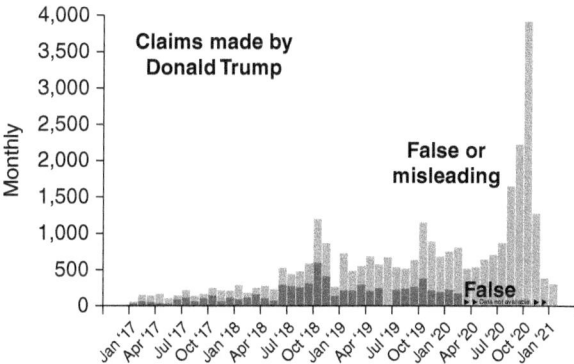

Data: "False or misleading claims" (The Washington Post) and "False claims"
(Daniel Dale, Toronto Star, later CNN).

www.ingramcontent.com/pod-product-compliance
Lightning Source LLC
Chambersburg PA
CBHW072148020426
42334CB00018B/1918